5-
4/24

TYPE

DESIGN, COLOR,
CHARACTER & USE

M I C H A E L B E A U M O N T

MICHAEL BEAUMONT

TYPE
DESIGN, COLOR, CHARACTER & USE

NORTH
LIGHT
BOOKS

Cincinnati, Ohio

A Quarto Book

Copyright © 1987 Quarto Publishing Plc
First published in the U.S.A. by
North Light Books, an imprint of
F&W Publications, Inc.
1507 Dana Avenue
Cincinnati, Ohio 45207

ISBN 0-89134-191-9

This book was designed and produced by
Quarto Publishing Plc
The Old Brewery, 6 Blundell Street,
London N7 9BH

Senior Editor Sandy Shepherd
Art Editor Gill Elsbury

Editors Hazel Harrison, Ricki Ostrov,
Eleanor van Zandt

Design Crucial Books, London
Design Assistant Iona McGlashan

Picture Researcher Penny Grant
Photographer John Wyand
Paste-up Patrizio Semproni

Art Director Moira Clinch
Executive Art Director Alastair Campbell
Editorial Director Carolyn King

Typeset by QV Typesetting Ltd and Text Filmsetters
Manufactured in Hong Kong by Regent Publishing
Services Ltd
Printed by Leefung-Asco Printer Ltd Hong Kong

CONTENTS

INTRODUCTION

I wrote this book with the typographer/designer and design student in mind, with the purpose of illustrating the infinite possibilities of using type creatively with color. However, I intended it to be of interest to all who are connected with, have an appreciation of, or wish to become acquainted with the visual communication industry in all its forms. There is something for everyone here: explanations of terminology, examples of the finest design work; how to determine type weight, leading and line spacing; and the market suitability of colors and typefaces for a range of designs — from logos on sweatshirts to billboard ads to corporate identity schemes. Throughout the book I've selected examples from well-known design groups and have analyzed their designs and use of type and color (and in some cases have taken the liberty of suggesting alternative designs).

You will see how tonal grays can be varied by using different typefaces on a page, by changing the size of the type in relationship to its format and by altering the interline spacing. We'll look into the reasons why some typefaces have excellent legibility whereas others are virtually unreadable. Sometimes the reason for illegibility is obvious, but in other instances it is not. For example, a designer might have chosen to have small white type reversed out of a black background, which looked perfect at the artwork stage where, as you would expect, quality was of the essence. But what was overlooked was the fact that the final product had to be reproduced on low-quality newsprint, and in the final result the high degree of ink absorption caused the delicate typographic characters to be filled in. " Obvious!" you may think, but it happens far too frequently.

I will also discuss the range of considerations that have to be made when choosing color, from the simple guidelines of the recessive nature of blue, and the dominant effect of bright reds and oranges, to the messages conveyed by different colors, to the subtlety of color associations with appropriate products and services.

The fact that one man in ten has some degree of colour blindness should also not be ignored. Although it would be impractical to design totally for this handicap, an understanding of its manifestations would benefit all designers involved with color choice. It is not particularly wise to specify one color to be overprinted with another color that is invisible to a sizeable proportion of the populace!

In general I've tried to present this book in direct, simple terms without either omitting important aspects of the subject, or insulting the intelligence of the professional with too many elementary examples. The book is intended as a working tool at every level and I hope that the many illustrative examples will inspire all designers and typographers, whatever their level of experience.

Michael Beaumont

TYPE
Making it work for you

Part One: **Introduction**

I have divided this book into two sections because it seemed logical to deal with typography and the black letter form first, and then to proceed to the ways in which color affects type and works together with it to put across a message.

In this part, I start with the basics by looking at type purely as an abstract form and the ways in which its shapes can be manipulated. This is followed by a series of guidelines on how to choose the most appropriate typeface for any particular job. I then go on to explain how to achieve an extensive value range within type. Part One concludes with demonstrations of type used with different colors with comments on why the examples do and don't work.

For the benefit of the non-typographer I feel that a list of basic terminology would be useful within this section. (For a more thorough and detailed list of typographic procedures and terms there is both an extensive appendix and a glossary at the back of the book.) A knowledge of these few terms will enable you to grasp the jargon with a greater degree of fluency than you had before and so increase your enjoyment of this book. So, here are some elementary terms that cover the styles and characteristics of the basic letter form.

Type size refers to the overall depth of the typeface, and includes a measure of space above and below the actual letter form, which corresponds with the piece of metal on which the type character used to sit. It is not to be confused with either x-height or cap height. The measurement of the type size is denoted by *the point.*

There is another method of measuring type. Specified as *key size,* it is calculated by the height of the capital letters, instead of the overall depth of the characters. (It is important to note, however, that the ascenders of some typefaces actually rise above the line of the top of the cap height.) It is the ideal system for mixing different faces on the base line, and insures consistency of cap height.

Most typefaces are part of what is known as "type families." Each family is one basic design developed and modified in many ways to provide a greater choice and flexibility for the designer during the design process.

For example, if we take one of the most popular sans serif typefaces, *Univers,* we can see its development from the standard form into a huge range of variations, at the same time maintaining its original feel. These modifications are labeled according to standard terms (see table opposite).

We can then take the first nine examples a stage further by italicizing them. We now have 18 variations from one basic form. This can be extended still further by italicization, which would bring our total number of variations to 36. Further modifications are possible, depending upon typeface suitability, such as *Outline.* The advantage of all these variations to designers and typographers is that they allow them to create variety without producing a bewildering confusion of styles.

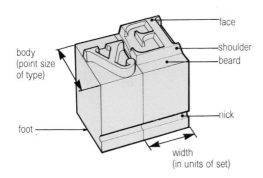

face
shoulder
beard
body (point size of type)
nick
foot
width (in units of set)

■ Type terminology derives from original setting in metal type.

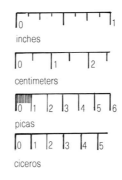

inches
centimeters
picas
ciceros

■ Differing methods for measuring type.

Roman

Italic

Serif

Sans Serif

■ Letters which stand up straight are called *Roman*, and those that slope forward are called *Italic*.
Almost all type can be categorized into two basic kinds of typeface - *Serif* and *Sans Serif*. The serif letter form is distinguished by a short stroke that projects from the ends of the character. Those letter forms without the short stroke are known as Sans Serif, from the French word *sans*, meaning without.

Light	*Light Italic*	* Ultra Light
Light Condensed	*Light Condensed Italic*	* Ultra Light Condensed
Light Expanded	*Light Italic Expanded*	* Ultra Light Expanded
Medium	*Medium Italic*	**Extra Bold**
Medium Condensed	*Medium Condensed Italic*	**Extra Bold Expanded**
Medium Expanded	*Medium Italic Expanded*	**Extra Bold Expanded**
Bold	***Bold Italic***	* **Ultra Bold**
Bold Condensed	***Bold Condensed Italic***	* **Ultra Bold Condensed**
Bold Expanded	***Bold Italic Expanded***	* **Ultra Bold Expanded**

* These examples are set in *Helvetica*, as the full range of styles was not available in *Univers*.

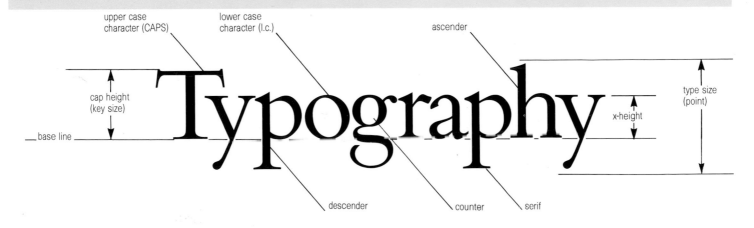

upper case character (CAPS)
lower case character (l.c.)
ascender
cap height (key size)
type size (point)
x-height
base line
descender
counter
serif

Typography

Forget the words – enjoy their shape

boo
lilli

Well, perhaps the professional designer shouldn't forget the words, but the sentiment is correct. Good typography is to do with shape, balance, and color. Always be aware of the shape your type makes. The use, or misuse, of the alphabet, could be the difference between failure and award-winning design.

But what is the alphabet? When you think about it, all that we have is a collection of abstract shapes which, when placed together in various combinations, convey messages that enable us to communicate with each other. Through the brilliant imaginations of type designers, many of these basic characters have become beautiful forms. With these shapes designers can create even more complicated and adventurous imagery, sometimes to resolve a graphic problem, other times purely as a fine art statement.

Bob Farber, who was until recently the art director of the *International Typeface Corporation's* journal, *U. & l.c.,* is one typographer who finds relaxation in treating type in this manner. By pursuing the very simple principles of repeat, mirror and reverse, Farber produced a series of colorful abstract images for the journal using only the basic letter forms of the alphabet.

Above One of the many considerations typographers encounter during their design work is how to deal with the different shapes caused by various character combinations. In the above example of Avant Garde we have the two extremes: consecutive round and consecutive vertical stress characters. When vertical characters occur together in a word extra space needs to be placed between them and when round characters occur together the space between them is reduced.

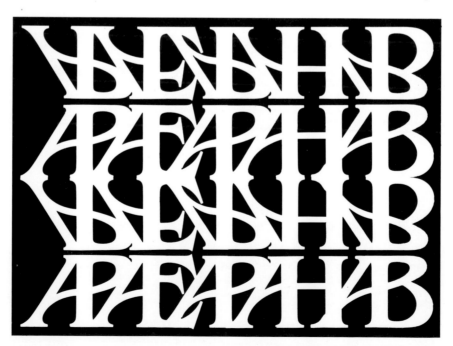

Left Bob Farber's creative design using mirrored characters from the ITC typeface, Benguiat.

I have included three of his designs. One of them, a striking example, was used for the front cover of one of the *ITC* journals. *ITC's* own description of the piece went as follows:

TYPE AS ART AS FUN.
Sometimes the most fun is enjoyed doing something you are not supposed to do. Ask any child, if you don't recall your own childhood. Bob Farber, one of our truly great problem solvers with type is quick to tell you, type is meant to be read. That's why he's had so much fun creating typographic images that not only can't be read but aren't intended for reading.

Here he's taken some of the logos or variant characters from the ITC Benguiat family and lined them up like Narcissus at the edge of the stream. Narcissus, you recall, was that Greek lad who so admired himself that he spent much of his time looking at his image in the water. The gods punished (rewarded?) his vanity by turning him into a streamside flower nodding towards its reflection.

Just as the narcissus is a thing of beauty, so is this inter-laced and multiple mirrored set of letters. You can identify the individual letters, but why bother? Just let your eyes feast on the flowing, joyous curves and the shapes they form."

Edward Gottschall: Editor

The addition of basic primary and secondary colors to a black and white design can produce equally vibrant results, as shown by the kaleidoscopic "A" on the right (it's so basic — just seven *ITC Serif Gothic* letter A's in a circle).

But good design does not have to be complex. What could be simpler than the double *ITC Century* "Y" shown (right)?

Such design concepts make ideal projects for newcomers to typography, enabling them to become acquainted with the practice of simultaneously handling color and the typographic

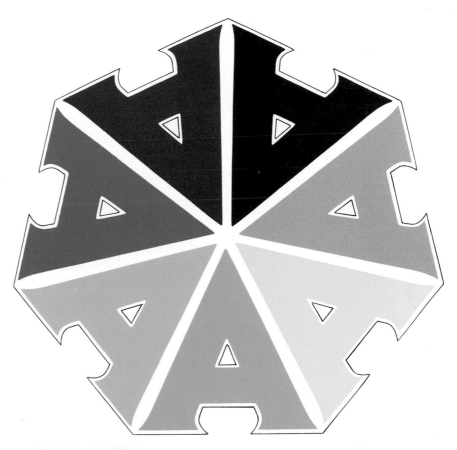

■ **Above** The second example of Bob Farber's creativity uses the ITC typeface Serif Gothic.

■ **Left** This third example illustrates the simple but effective use of the letter Y from the ITC Century typeface.

form without having to worry at all about the restrictions normally encountered in everyday studio situations.

CALLIGRAPHY

Moving back in time you will find that there is nothing new in the marriage between art and typography. In oriental cultures calligraphy is a highly esteemed art form, based on centuries of tradition, fully integrated with other artistic skills and traditions.

The term calligraphy simply means beautiful writing, although its beauty does depend very much on the eye of the beholder, or personal taste. Just as many styles of art exist today, from the exceptionally clean and tight to the totally free and abstract, so it is with calligraphy.

Modern calligraphy has a definitely formal basis in the traditions of the Romans and early Christians. During the period of the Roman Empire our standard alphabet was developed and transmitted to the conquered lands of Europe and, subsequently, developed by the teaching of Christianity.

The Romans adopted the following characters from the Greek alphabet — A B E H I K M N O T X Y Z — without modification, and remodeled the following — C D G L P R S — to suit their own language. With the re-introduction of F, Q and V, previously discarded by the Greeks, virtually all our present-day alphabet existed, with only J, U and W to be added at a later date. By the early days of Christianity the Romans had established not just this formal alphabet, but several variations of writing, including the introduction of the serif.

By the early fourth century AD the Romans had developed a new script, the uncial, which became

■ **Above** The shape of the characters in this Roman inscription derived initially from the brush strokes that were used to paint preliminary designs. Later they were modified by the chisel as letter forms were cut into stone. Serifs owe much to the directional action of the chisel.

abcdefghijk
lmnopqrst
uvwxyz
1234567890
œ?!£$(.,;:)

■ **Above** The American Uncial typeface is based upon the original alphabets developed by the Romans in the early fourth century AD.

■ **Right** This example of a sixteenth-century manuscript is attractively enclosed in solidly colored and richly designed borders surrounding the text.

the main face of the early writings. With the inclusion of both descenders and ascenders, our present-day upper and lower case emerged (the typeface American Uncial far left below, is based on these early styles).

By the tenth century, through the influence of the Church, all the elements of modern writing were in evidence. There followed a tremendously rich period in the development of illumination that has left a wonderful legacy of letter forms and scripts.

Today these same calligraphic skills are being revived, not so much as a commercial trade (although there are professional calligraphers), but more as an art form. The exciting aspect of present-day calligraphy is the tremendous variety of styles and media with which it is executed — as I'm sure you'll agree from the examples shown.

As you can see from the development within the examples here, it has become increasingly difficult — not that it really matters — to see where callig-

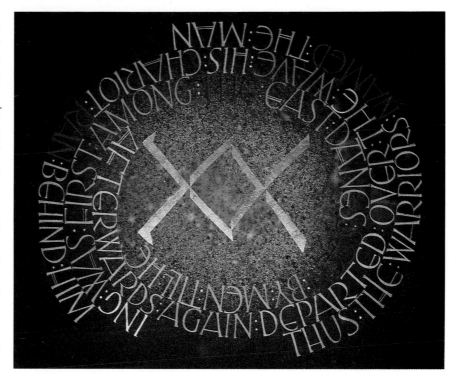

Left A lovely example of calligraphic technique by the American artist Georgia Deaver. She has cleverly set up a contrast between the freedom of the title and the tight control and condensed style of the body copy. Notice too how each character in the title sits above each column, but by allowing the flourishes to extend beyond their parameters she has prevented the columns from becoming too strong and unbalancing the design.

Above This effective combination of different motifs written with a quill in silver and gold leaf and gouache is stylistically similar to the Bob Farber examples on the preceding pages.

of layout and design that can be achieved by the skillful manipulation of those same letter forms.

Typographer *David Harris* designed a particular face, which he called *Musisca*. It is an excellent example of how the art of calligraphy can be developed into a formal script combining the freedom of the hand-drawn letter together with the control of a formal typeface.

David also created an attractive wordset on the theme "The Fellowship of the Round Table" using his *Musisca* typeface (shown left).

COUNTER SHAPES

Returning to our theme "Forget the words — enjoy their shape," it is always important to consider not just the shape that the individual characters or words create but the spaces around and within those actual shapes. Look carefully at the shape of the lower case *Helvetica* "s," (shown below).

If we close in on the character, reverse it from black to white and spin it through 90°, we become aware of what looks like a new image. But it is not really new; it is only the relationship of black to white and position of the letter that has altered.

SHAPING LOGOS

The art of the hand-drawn letter form is often applied to logotype design. Even those faces based on the sans serif form often contain elements of hand drawing to achieve that little bit extra in terms of a unique statement. It is always interesting

■ When Letraset want to promote one of their new typefaces they often ask the designer to produce a "wordset" to illustrate how they see their initial concept working in terms of words and their shapes. "The Fellowship of the Round Table" is a wordset designed by typographer David Harris in his own Musisca typeface. "Victorian Bridge Building" is designed by Tony Geddes in his own creation, Senator Display, and the third example, "American Cars of the 50s" is in Vegas, designed by David Quay.

raphy ends, and conventional typographic letter forms begin. In many respects it is a natural progression from one to the other.

DRY TRANSFER LETTERS

The advent of the dry transfer letter form has, to a large extent, helped to bring together calligraphy and the more formal typefaces, giving designers the facility to achieve their visual aspirations with greater speed and efficiency. As a means of illustrating the infinite variety of design that can be created from "rub-down" letter forms, Letraset, the British graphic arts company and producers of transfer lettering, often commissions the finest typographers to design new typefaces in dry transfer and to demonstrate the wonderful range

Below This is another effective use of contrast, this time by Tim Girvin Design in Seattle, done for Cannon Productions. The word "CERTAIN," which is set in a Perpetua derivative, provides a foil for the violence and freedom of the brush lettering below it.

Right This colorful logo design for Heal's, the British furniture store, was based on the typeface Frutiger, a Gill Sans derivative. The designers – Minale, Tattersfield & Partners – have introduced basic geometric shapes, which symbolize the idea of home-building.

Above The logotype for W Photo is a good example of how the space between the characters can be used just as effectively as the characters themselves.

CAMARGUE

Left The company Richard Yates Architects Inc. has successfully used a motif of building blocks to form the letter Y associated with the firm and to symbolize the nature of its business.

Above Minale, Tattersfield & Partners were also the designers of this logotype for a range of fashion accessories which was marketed under the name of Camargue, an area of France famed for its white horses. The silhouette of a horse's head has been used to form the character C. The horse's body has been allowed to partially cover the A, forming the bar of the letter, without detracting from legibility. The typeface is a modified Fritz Quadra.

Left This award-winning design by the Seattle company, Tim Girvin Design, illustrates just how free and decorative typography can be without losing any of its promotional function. It was produced for Bloomingdale's, the famous New York department store, and Tim Girvin himself was the calligrapher.

Above and right These images illustrate an interesting calligraphic technique used on a record sleeve for the jazz musician Gerry Mulligan. It involved loading a large brush with ink and applying it to low-weight tracing paper, which caused crinkling.

Right This detail of an award-winning full-page advertisement for British Airways was part of a four-part alphabet produced by the London branch of the advertising agency, Foote, Cone & Belding. Apart from the delightful letters they have created it's also an excellent example of page layout and how to work type around unusual shapes, and the tonal color of the body copy is just the right size and weight. The art direction and typography was by Steve Grime, and the illustrations were done by Paul Sample.

Far right Old Style wooden display type, much used before the days of photographic headlines, can also produce interesting imagery, especially when the blocks are under-inked and cause the ink to break up.

to see what methods different designers use when they approach logotype design. Each has his or her own style and way of working, but more often than not there will be a common approach of logic and development to the work.

CREATIVE TYPEFACES

As you've seen from some of the calligraphic examples, type does not have to be either rigid or formal. There are many ways of creating exciting typography from whatever materials and media you think fit. For instance, interesting textures can be made by painting with ink and then allowing the paper to wrinkle, or by deliberately under-inking old-style wooden display type. This page provides a few ideas.

Right Another example of a fun typeface, this time a personal greetings card I produced recently for my own family.

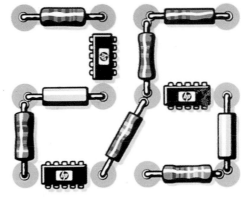

HEWLETT·PACKARD LTD

YEARS OF COMMITMENT

Left A simple but effective design to commemorate 25 years of business in the United Kingdom for the international computer company Hewlett-Packard. It was produced for the company by the London design group The Partners, and contrasts a simple condensed sans serif face with the freedom of the numerals, constructed from computer components.

Above This two-color typographic design was created by Grundy & Northedge to advertise a "Medical Equipment Design Award" bursary scheme. It cleverly incorporates images from medical technology.

Right The design for this invitation to an art exhibition called Dutch Crossing uses an interesting combination of wax resist and woodcut letters. The number 3 stands for the 3 artists whose work was presented, and the letter W for the Watermans gallery where the exhibition took place.

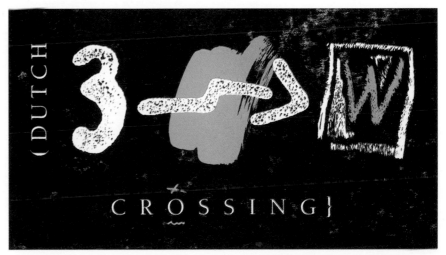

Having looked closely at various methods of creating type in an extremely free and imaginative way we'll now move toward the other extreme — tight control by means of camera distortion and graphics modification.

MODIFYING TYPE

The re-proportioning of type is now very common but sadly often abused. Headline machines and most modern computer typesetters can condense,

expand, italicize and back slant, but if the designer is lacking in his or her feel for typographic proportion, the result is imbalance and appalling proportions of type characters.

As you will no doubt appreciate, one of the major factors of good type design is the relationship between the weight of the *stem* (vertical) and *bar* (horizontal) of the letter form. As soon as you start to distort the character by either electronic or photographic means, the relationship between the

■ **Right** The following examples of the word "Typography" have been set in Univers medium and electronically modified on a Linotron 202 computer typesetter.

Typography
No modification

Typography
No modification

Typography
Expanded by 20%

Typography
Condensed by 20%

Typography
Expanded by 40%

Typography
Condensed by 40%

Typography
Condensed by 60%

Typography
Expanded by 60%

stem and bar will alter and, depending on the actual typeface, there will come a point when the balance between the two is wrong. In the examples shown below notice the point where the visual relationship between the stem and bar suffers, making the distortion increasingly unacceptable. Just compare the distorted type with the true designs of *condensed, expanded and italic.*

Of course this doesn't mean that you shouldn't modify type but it is important that you be dis-

cerning. Large headlines can often come out stronger with just a nudge here and there.

There is another machine available to the designer that can be extremely useful, especially when designing logos. It is generally known as a graphics modifier and has the ability to outline, inline, and drop shadow in whatever combinations you require. Because of its mechanical base it is accurate and produces uniformity of line.

Standard Korinna Extra Bold

With drop shadow

With box line

With double outline

With double outline plus decorative screen.

Typography

No modification

Typography

10% Slant

Typography

20% Slant

Typography

30% Slant

Typography

True Univers medium condensed

Typography

Electronically condensed Univers

Typography

True Univers medium expanded

Typography

Electronically expanded Univers

Typography

True Univers medium italic

Typography

Electronically italicized Univers

Above right Compare the true Univers with the electronically modified version. Note how the basic character of the type is distorted and lost. The greater the modification the greater the degree of "bastardization" of the original, leading to unacceptable standards of typographic form and taste.

There are times, however, when you may want to distort a typeface deliberately — sometimes uniformly, other times in a totally free manner. Some headline machines are equipped with a spe- cial lens that allows you to set type in circles, in a dip-arch movement or to create a balloon effect. Box perspective is also possible, as are converging perspective and general distortions.

■ The possibilities of distorting typefaces to create different effects by using special lenses, computers and other techniques are almost limitless. This page provides just a few examples.

Herb Lubalin

This chapter would not be complete without examples of one of the greatest typographic masters of our time, the American typographer *Herb Lubalin*. He produced numerous designs for countless clients, far too many to include in one small section of any book. Some of these designs are well known but, as with any form of real art, you can't see them too often. Words from me would be superfluous, so just "enjoy their shape."

■ Herb Lubalin's designs are world-famous and he is known particularly for his imaginative use of letters and ideas. In the design "Oh! Ah!" he used the initials of the photographer Anthony Hyde and his representative Li-Lian Oh as a means of introducing them to their prospective clients. The Grumbacher logo was designed for the company of that name, which sells art materials. "Mother & Child," probably Lubalin's most famous piece and the designer's own personal favorite was, ironically, for a magazine that was never published. The design "Avant Garde" was originally a masthead for the magazine of the same name, but led Lubalin to develop an entirely new typeface – Avant Garde Gothic.

Why can't I use Gill Sans Extra Bold Condensed?

Countless typefaces have been developed over the years, particularly over the last two decades, because creative designers are continually seeking new and more exciting ways of creating mood and impact. Choosing the correct typeface can be a daunting task for the inexperienced designer — where to start? what size? what weight? and oh, those type catalogs! There are literally thousands of faces to choose from, which can make the whole process all so intimidating. It can at times be something of a major task for even the most experienced designer to produce something different, so what chance has the novice typographer? This vast range of type styles often has differences so minute that experienced typographers have to look twice to spot the subtle variations. So what is the answer?

The first thing is not to panic! Most experienced designers will restrict their choice of faces to no more than a dozen or so working styles, although even this can lead to an exceptionally large choice when all the family variations are taken into account.

CATEGORIES OF TYPEFACES

When building a basic library, look for variation and contrast. The simplest approach to achieving this objective is to study how the various typefaces are categorized and what the basic groupings are. The identifying characteristics of most typefaces can be grouped into six easily-understood categories. Along with modifications of the former, another four are created.

When compiling a working list of faces it is a good idea to include a range of examples from each of the various groupings. A basic working list could look something like that below and on the opposite page.

The six basic typefaces are: Old Style Serif; Modern Serif; Square Serif; Sans Serif; Scripts; and Stylistic/Novelty. The four modifications are: Modified Sans Serif; Outline/Inline; Connecting Scripts; and Non-Connecting Scripts.

With the exception of some of the script examples, all the examples shown contain the normal variations of light, bold, condensed, italic, etc. These nineteen examples provide not just an excellent foundation for the beginner, but a sound working basis for the professional designer, too.

OLD STYLE SERIF

Caslon

Garamond

Plantin

MODERN SERIF

Bodoni

Century Schoolbook

Tiffany

SQUARE SERIF

Clarendon

Egyptian

Rockwell

SANS SERIF

Univers

Futura

Gill Sans

MODIFIED SANS SERIF

Optima

Souvenir Gothic

Baker Signet

CONNECTING SCRIPT

Brush Script

English Script

NON-CONNECTING SCRIPT

Zapf Chancery

Medici Script

sculptured *type*

How many ways can you draw the letters of the alphabet? The great type designers of today have been creating major works of art that look like sculptures out of these letters. Those shown here are just a small portion of the kinds of letter-forms that can be found. There are many more just waiting to be discovered. "Sculptured" type—there's no end to these wonderful works of art.

A GALLIARD ULTRA ITALIC B VELJOVIC BLACK ITALIC C FENICE ULTRA ITALIC D GALLIARD BOLD E BENGUIAT BOOK F ISBELL BOLD G USHERWOOD BLACK ITALIC H BENGUIAT MEDIUM CONDENSED I ISBELL HEAVY J BARCELONA BOLD K ISBELL MEDIUM L ZAPF CHANCERY BOLD M GALLIARD BLACK N GALLIARD ULTRA ITALIC O NOVARESE BOLD ITALIC P NOVARESE BOLD ITALIC Q AVANT GARDE BOOK R GALLIARD ROMAN S CUSHING MEDIUM T NEWTEXT REGULAR U VELJOVIC BLACK ITALIC V VELJOVIC BOLD W NOVARESE BOLD ITALIC X ISBELL HEAVY ITALIC Y ISBELL MEDIUM Z ISBELL BOLD ITALIC

DESIGNED BY ROBERT WAKEMAN

TYPOGRAPHIC INNOVATIONS
246 WEST 38 STREET
NEW YORK 10018
PHONE 764-6464

A Galliard Ultra Italic **B** Veljovic Black Italic **C** Fenice Ultra Italic **D** Galliard Bold **E** Benguiat Book **F** Isbell Bold **G** Usherwood Black Italic **H** Benguiat Medium Condensed **I** Isbell Heavy **J** Barcelona Bold **K** Isbell Medium **L** Zapf Chancery Bold **M** Galliard Black **N** Galliard Ultra Italic **O** Novarese Bold Italic **P** Novarese Bold Italic **Q** Avant Garde Book **R** Galliard Roman **S** Cushing Medium **T** Newtext Regular **U** Veljovic Black Italic **V** Veljovic Bold **W** Novarese Bold Italic **X** Isbell Heavy Italic **Y** Isbell Medium **Z** Isbell Bold Italic

Once you have become fully conversant with a basic, if slightly limited range of faces, it is a fairly easy matter to extend your vocabulary as your confidence grows.

CHARACTERISTICS OF THE BASIC TYPE FAMILIES

You must appreciate that the situations suggested for each type of category are generalizations only. Rules are made to be broken and the only real consideration is "If it looks right, it is right."

Old Style Serif: Caslon

The characteristics of the Old Style Serif include a boldness and strength of feature with relatively uniform stroke widths. The serifs normally join the stem with a curve, and the letters are generally of open proportion. In their light and medium styles they are easy to read. This makes them highly suitable for use in books and other forms of literature in which there are large blocks of text.

Modern Serif: Century

Unlike the Old Style Serif, in this face there is a strong contrast between thick and thin strokes, with little or no bracketing (the curve that links the serif to the stem). The weight stress of the Modern Serif in round letters is symmetrically located. This category is also known as Transitional Style. It, too, can be used for book text although the bold members of this family are better suited to shorter passages of text such as those found in ads and leaflets.

Square Serif: Rockwell

The main feature of this category is the strong, heavily blocked design of the serif, with little contrast between the vertical and horizontal strokes. The serifs join the main stem at a sharp angle or with a small radius. Unlike the previous two examples, square serifs rarely create the right appearance in extensive text matter. They are much more suited to advertising where mood and expression are of far greater importance.

Sans Serif: Unica

The strokes of this face tend to be visually equal in weight, and geometric designs are common. The simplicity of design in this group lends itself to large family variations, from ultra light through ultra bold. It is therefore the most versatile of all the categories – with the exception of large volumes of text, where its vertical stress can be tiring on the eyes – it can work well in any situation.

Stylistic/Novelty: Neue Lutherische Fraktur

This category usually applies to any typeface not fitting any of the previous headings. They are unique and highly distinctive, often consisting of decorative designs that create impact, mood or special effects. They work better in large sizes because of their intricate design features and are normally used for single words only or in very short phrases.

Modified Sans Serif: Optima

Although Sans Serif in appearance, the Modified Sans Serif design contains either small flared strokes or minute serifs, along with the greater variation and contrast between the thick and thin strokes that are typical of the serif faces. Not quite as versatile as the basic sans serif, and better suited to larger areas of text because the small flare of the suggested serif reduces vertical stress and thus aids readability.

Outline/Inline:
Times Modern Black Outline

These designs are, very often, created from existing typefaces that have been modified by outlines, inlines, shadows, contours or a combination of any of these features. They are restricted mainly to headlines and product names.

Connecting Scripts: English Script

This group of modifications emulates the cursive writing of calligraphy and the natural flow of handwriting. Although it has the consistency of type design it is not normally suitable for text setting because the designs are usually of pen or brushstroke origin. They often work well on packaging and other forms of "below the line" material.

Non-Connecting Scripts:
Zapf Chancery

A great deal of variety is contained within this group; it includes both non-connecting hand-drawn letter forms and ornate, formal typefaces. The designs can be based on pen- or brushwork, black letter, informal scripts or elaborate designs. Legibility can suffer with some of these designs, particularly with the black letter variations, and these should be used with care. These scripts are used in the same cases as those of the connecting scripts.

■ **Below** This detail from a poster designed by Robert Wakeman, for Graphic Technology, displays a range of faces, all of which can be used in a corporate design, depending on the image the company wants to put across.

SUITING THE FACE TO THE PRODUCT

Much of the art of choosing the correct typeface and weight lies in the combination of product association with the designer's aesthetic judgment. For example, to promote jewelry, a designer would consider a choice of delicate faces, probably a fine serif or an italic. For directional signs or commands such as *Keep Left, Stop,* etc., a strong sans serif face in its semi-bold or bold style would be more suitable. Then there's typography to advertise engineering products. Because the face needs to suggest strength and power, delicate serifs are less appropriate than a stronger square serif such as *Rockwell Bold* or *Clarendon Medium.*

Above and right In these examples, the message is clear and uncluttered. The generous use of space around the words in both cases ensures readability, and the design touches are delightfully humorous, with clever use made of a giraffe's neck in the F.

Above Jewson is a leading British firm of lumber and builders' supplies. The inspiration and starting point for their logo was a carpenter's rule, which creates a solid, strong typeface, appropriate to the nature of their industry.

Left The logo script on this hair-care packaging was designed by Trickett & Webb for a company called John Frieda. The script with its ribbon motif gives a personal touch and an upmarket image.

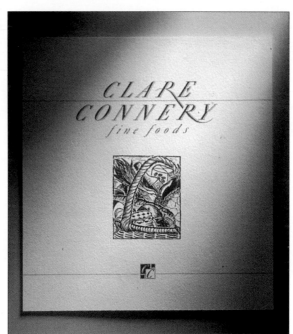

Above This design, by Coley, Porter, Bell, was done for Clare Connery, the Irish celebrity cook, as part of a design scheme for her chain of delicatessens in Belfast. Notice the fine decorative use of the leg on the R.

Above The Rockwell typeface, although strong, has a cluttered look because of its heavy serifs. If a basic sans serif had been used, such as Helvetica, it would have been far more successful, as the extra white space would have increased legibility and impact.

■ **Above and above left** An interesting comparison can be seen in the faces used on these delivery vans. In the Thorntons example, the van livery has been properly thought out and works well, while the Federal Express livery is a rather clumsy attempt at trying to suggest speed of operation, using the italic double S. However, it fails to do so because the typography as a whole has a heavy, static quality.

■ **Left and above** Yet another example of excellent design work from Minale, Tattersfield & Partners. Just as the Jewson logo suggests building and construction, this one shouts out "confectionery," even to those who do not know that Thorntons are makers of high-quality chocolates. The color and the flowing script both send messages of delicious sweetness, which are reinforced by the decorative geometric shapes sitting beneath the script.

Right and below Two interesting approaches to page layout. The Pentagram piece, right, is typical of a situation where numerous illustrations and ample text have to be placed within a limited area. By positioning the map centrally and working the other elements around it the designer has kept the layout fresh and uncluttered. The captions are set in a smaller size than the text, which creates a good tonal contrast. This is further strengthened by the use of tints. The example below, an annual report to company staff designed by Trickett & Webb, uses two-color printing only. White space has been used well, and the designer has spaced out the main title effectively. Notice also the nice touch of the raised initial A to begin the main text.

SUITABLE FACES

When determining suitable typefaces for running text you can't really lay down rules, only basic guidelines. Generally speaking, medium weight serif faces work better than sans faces. This is due to their greater horizontal stress, which guides the eye effortlessly across the page.

For captions and callouts, try and choose a face that contrasts with the text style; for example, if the running text is set in a medium serif, consider sans, italic, or condensed faces, or a heavier weight, which will stand out against the body text.

There are not really any correct or incorrect faces for running text, since the color of all typefaces can be changed fundamentally to improve legibility by varying line and character spacing.

■ **Left** The box for Dorma "Jenny Wren" comforters (duvets), designed by Trickett & Webb, is a good example of how proportionately small the product description and company name can become without weakening the message. If the type were to be larger in this case the message would become crude and ugly.

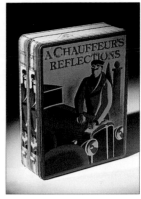

■ **Above** Trickett & Webb used a 1920s poster design and 1940s book cover design for a product range of "Men's gifts." In the example above, the driver's cap clips the type without affecting legibility. In the adjacent example, however, the placing of the white lettering of the word "outfit" against the cream background has undoubtedly reduced its legibility.

■ **Left** Typography is subject to fashion just as any other form of design is, as can be seen by these two poster designs from The Partners. The lefthand image is clean, modern and dramatic, creating its mood by the use of photography and the colors black, white and red.The righthand image typifies a current interest in typography, design and illustration from the 1950s.

MIXING TYPEFACES

Once you have committed a basic selection of faces to memory, the next stage is to combine the various styles in a cohesive and controlled manner. If you stick to using variations within a single family grouping you will always be safe in the knowledge that they are compatible. But how do you successfully combine different faces from other family groups without losing continuity of design and good taste? The easiest way to approach this design problem is to start by combining opposites. A standard sans serif such as *Gill Sans, Helvetica,* or *Univers,* will blend with virtually any serif face, whereas you would not use *Helvetica* with *Univers* or another similar sans serif. They are far too close in style to work.

Within the vast range of serif typefaces, many are quite compatible, and it is often needless to resort to finding their opposite in another face. Their contrasting design features add color and life to a design when they are combined. Most of the square serifs work well with the modern serifs such as *Times* and *Baskerville.*

The various areas of design where typeface mixing works well can be simplified quite easily.

Advertising: The most common form of mixing in advertising is for the headline to be set in a strong sans serif face with the text in a suitable book, or text, face. The Old Style *Garamond* is a popular text choice, and so are the moderns like *Baskerville* and *Century.* This combination can also work well in reverse, when you use a strong serif for the headline followed by sans serif text, although it is less common. Depending upon the style of the advertisement, virtually any weight of typeface can be used for the headline, but with the text, or body copy, there does come a point where legibility suffers if the weight and tonal color of the type go beyond a certain level. This point of reduced

legibility can only be assessed in the context of the advertisement and its relationship to the rest of the design.

Many ads, particularly those concerned with trade magazines, contain reader reply coupons. This is another area of design where a change of typeface can add contrast and variety. In these coupons a possible third typeface is often incorporated when the company's name and address have a specific style or face. But do beware — there are few occasions when more than two family types work well within one design. When you consider the variations of weight and italicization within any one group there is plenty of choice without having to use faces from other groups.

It takes up to 40 dumb animals to make a fur coat.

But only one to wear it.

If you don't want millions of animals tortured and killed in leg-hold traps, don't buy a fur coat.

LYNX
Fighting the fur trade
PO Box 509 Dunmow, Essex. Tel: 0371 2016

■ **Right** This poster of the ballet dancer Baryshnikov illustrates how creative mixing can be introduced into the minimum of copy: different styles of type have been used within just one word. The choice of a simple sans for the remaining text gives just the right balance – a serif could have been distracting. The poster was designed by Bob Appleton of Appleton Design for the Hartford Ballet.

■ **Above** Type mixing is not all that common on billboards because there is usually relatively little copy. When it does occur it is often used to contrast the logotype with the main typeface, as in this stunning example for Greenpeace. The art direction was by Jeremy Pemberton of the Yellowhammer agency.

Billboard & Poster: If you were to distinguish between the billboard and the information poster you would find that the billboard is not normally a vehicle for type mixing. There is a general rule for billboards which says that the copy headline should be restricted to a short, crisp phrase of no more than nine words. The reasoning behind this is quite simple: most billboard sites are positioned along roads or highways, to be viewed by passing motorists who will have time to see only short, swift messages.

Type mixing can work on a billboard, but usually only when a word or the product logo is combined within the headline for effect or emphasis. There are, however, billboard sites such as bus and rail stations, pedestrian precincts and underpasses in positions frequented by pedestrians. In such situations copywriters have the opportunity to develop ideas that often result in a humorous approach aimed at bringing some light relief to waiting passengers and passing pedestrians. As with general advertising the combination of a headline in one face followed by the text in another, can work well.

The purpose of a poster tends to be more informative than that of the larger billboard. Public service announcements, health information, theater and film promotions are typical of its uses. More often than not it will appear indoors or in public places where people have time to read and digest its contents. This allows the designer the opportunity of providing the reader with a greater degree of information and the typographer greater scope for creativity. The same guidelines apply to poster layout as to advertising layout.

Corporate Identity: This type of brief is not really the occasion for exploiting a variety of weights and styles of typeface, but there is some room for a little variation within a corporate scheme. This frequently takes the form of a specific design for the company logo, often hand-drawn, beside a contrasting typeface for the address and general information details.

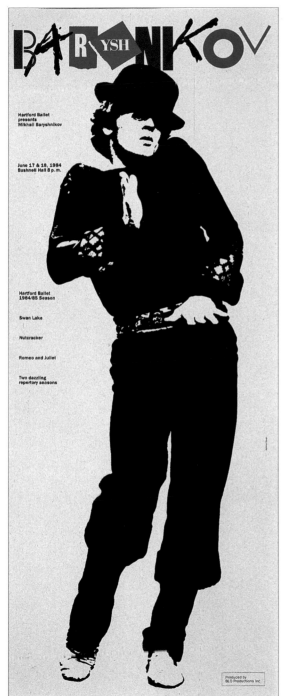

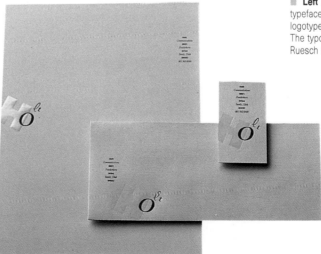

■ **Above and left** These two examples illustrate ways of mixing different sans serif typefaces. The Imperial War Museum motif is a hand-drawn sans serif face designed as a logo for the museum by The Partners. The logo was then developed further by Grundy & Northedge to act as a brochure cover and letterhead for the museum's forthcoming festival.

■ **Left** This interesting mixture of typefaces and color formed a logotype for Holt Communications. The typographer was Daniel Ruesch of Tandem Studios.

Print: General literature, brochure and illustrated book design are areas where the mixing of various typefaces is not only most common but also desirable. The general text is often set in a light, book serif style with introductory paragraphs in a heavier weight. Where subheadings occur they can be set in a different face, usually a sans serif, as can be the main headings. Callouts would nor-

mally be set in a basic sans serif such as *Helvetica* or *Univers,* or perhaps *News Gothic* if a slightly more condensed feel is desired. It's surprising how small a size of callout is readable; 6pt is quite common. A change of style is definitely a good idea for illustrative captioning. Sometimes an italic version of the main text is used for captions, but the italic might already have been incorporated within the main body to add clarity and emphasis to a particular point. For that reason it is nearly always preferable to move away from the main text style and choose a complementary sans serif face for the captions. A change of face can also work well within the body copy when a change of emphasis or illustrative point is being made outside the general flow or context of the main text.

The general guidelines in the above examples can easily be applied to all the other areas of visual communication. In every one of them balance, contrast, legibility and visual interest are essential criteria.

TYPE VARIATIONS

To conclude this chapter it is worth making the point that typefaces are not always what they seem. It is surprising how many variations there are within the same face from supplier to supplier. Some manufacturers use only the original artwork licensed by the owner, whereas others create their own version of the more popular faces. Often, when a face is redrawn the name will also change. *Haas Helvetica,* for example, from the German *Haas Foundry,* has undergone subtle modifications since it became available under licence. The *Scangraphic* company's version is called *Europa Grotesk,* the company *Varityper* uses the name *Megaron, Compugraphic* uses the term *Helios* for its film fonts and now the name *Triumvirate* for its CRT machines, and *Berthold* calls its version *Akzidenz-Grotesk.*

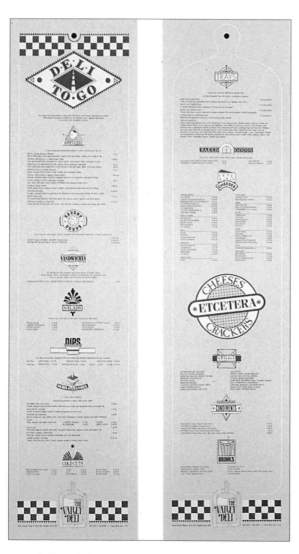

■ **Right** Menus always give designers an opportunity for creativity, and this example – from Steven Wedeen of Vaughn, Wedeen Creative, Inc. – is no exception. Each course is separated by an appropriate logo, which adds life and fun to the basic concept, and the final result lacks nothing in spite of the fact that only two-color printing was used.

BY WILLIAM MONTALBANO

CHINA

Every now and then, with the tried patience of a bureaucracy scorned, the Chinese government issues a startling appeal to the peasants of northern China: "Please return the Great Wall".

The official concern is not hard to understand. Neither is the fact that it goes unheeded, given the priorities of poor peasants who live with the wall for a neighbor.

These last 2,200 years, the wall has been an awesome symbol of Chinese nationhood: a 4,000-mile tribute to the audacity—and the myopia—of the society that conceived it. Emperor Qin Shie Huang, who first unified China, ordered the wall, and so it was built at a reputed cost of one million lives. Secondary to its grandeur in the mind of China and in the judgment of history is the mundane fact that as a defensive barrier the wall never worked. Over the centuries the barbarians it was designed to keep out streamed across with depressing regularity.

Such niceties are lost entirely on the peasants of north China—poor people historically rooted to the soil and calculatingly remote from central authority. The wall represents a bonanza, a rock quarry of truly legendary proportions. Over the centuries, the bricks hewn by the emperor's legions have found second hand employment in uncounted thousands of peasant homes: as wall and door lintels, as floors and ovens, even—God forbid the emperor should find out—as pig sties.

1500-1027 BC
The Shang
Dynasty. First
dynasty in
China's
recorded
history.
Bronze ritual
wine vessel
(shown)
becomes high
art form.

1027-221 BC
Zhou Dynasty.
Confucius born
551 BC
Halley's comet
regularly
observed.
Mathematics
developed.

I first wrote about the vanishing wall several years ago as a correspondent based in Peking. I was amused, but hardly surprised, to read a few months ago of yet another appeal from the same government to the same stolid peasants to return what they have borrowed from mankind. In the interim, obviously, some new pigs had found shelter among old stones.

There is, mind you, no insolence implicit in pillaging the wall, or any rebellion inherent among the peasants in their refusal to bring it back. It is, rather, a practical matter. Well-lined ovens, wind-resistant walls and eusseted pigs make for healthier and happier families. First things first.

Such essential pragmatism among the people was one of the things that most struck me about life in China. Rulers go and come. So do emperors and revolutionaries, and landlords and cadres. Policies are made, unmade and remade. What was bad yesterday is good today but, careful, it may be unmentionable tomorrow. The impositions of authority, like the changing seasons that still dictate the rhythm of life for most of China's people, wax and then wane.

Amid such flux, though, there are some constants, traits and convictions ingrained over the centuries that seem virtually immune to changing circumstances and systems of government.

Pragmatism of the sort practiced by rock-hungry peasants ranks high on my own subjective list of the

8   9

Left This fine example of creative calligraphic techniques linked within a typographical layout comes from Pentagram UK. Notice how a second and third color and additional typefaces have been used as captions between the two main text columns.

Below From a two-column grid to a single-column structure. Paul Arden directed this double-page spread for Alexon's African fashion collection with photographs by Richard Avedon and typography from Roger Kennedy of Saatchi & Saatchi. The large quantity of white space around the type area plus an above-average amount of spacing between lines all help to create the sophistication necessary to set off this stunning visual image.

This lack of standardization can cause problems, especially if creative requirements bring the designer into contact with a wide range of setting systems. The number of faces available will vary from manufacturer to manufacturer with most typesetters possessing only a selection from that range. This means that when designers prepare visuals they must take into account the typographic range of their local suppliers. Because of this variation of style from the different sources it's extremely important for the designer to have at hand the relevant type specimen sheets.

AVEDON ALEXON AFRICA

A

Yee hoo!, the old woman cries, as she butts the dancer gently in the belly. The dancer has been approved. The dancer is outstanding. The eye popping, limb contorting swirl of magic and colour that is the tribal dance of the Nomads of the Niger has reached its mesmeric climax. In a great white egg of a studio somewhere on New York's East Side, Richard Avedon the photographer who Truman Capote has called "The man with gifted eyes" breathes the tingling magic of the Wodaabe tribe into Alexon's African collection. Colours and primitive pattern woven into cloth, woven into clothes bring Alexon screeching into the now.

But gray *is* a color!

It really isn't sporting to puncture anyone's balloon, but when we read in a trade magazine that, last year alone, Americans spent $2.5 billion on bathrooms and bath-related facilities, we could only think, "Peanuts!" Compared with the attention some of our ancient antecedents paid to bathing and bath facilities, our recent expenditures for, and preoccupation with, bathrooms is just a drip in the tub.

Ancient baths. Five thousand years ago, a highly civilized society dwelling in the Indus Valley had sophisticated bathing equipment—a public bath that measured 24 x 40 feet, with a scientific drainage system, and private bathrooms in their homes with tubs, drains, spigots and faucets.

In the well-preserved palaces of Aegean civilizations, there are recognizable remnants of bathrooms with tubs, footbaths, drains and vertical pipes, proving that, as far back as 2,000 B.C., people were bathing with running water.

Whatever we know of Egyptian bathing habits comes from early writings, and pertains to rituals for priests, who were required to wash four times a day in cold water.

Ancient Sumerians, too, were known to have had bathing facilities.

But it was Mosaic Law, found in the Bible in Leviticus (16,17) and Numbers (19), that first firmly associated washing and bathing with religious duty. Since the germ-theory of disease was still a long way off, it is not certain whether the washing rites were inspired by a devotion to cleanliness or Godliness, but "purification" was the objective. Dozens of ritual washings are spelled out in the Bible. Among

Some did it for cleanliness. Some did it for Godliness. Some did it for sport. Some did it for pleasure. For one reason or another, for 5,000 years, civilized people have been "turned on" to

ILLUSTRATION BY GINI SHURTLEFF

bathtubs

the more common practices among orthodox Jews are the required hand-washing before meals and the ritual bath for women, the mikvah, before marriage and following menses. There is no mention of required baths for menfolk, but who says life is fair?

The Greeks. The Greeks of ancient times needed no motivation for bathing except for sheer pleasure. They frolicked in tubs of polished stone, marble or wood—first in cold water, then in warm. Bathing, for them, was a purely social and recreational activity in esthetic surroundings.

Orientals. Although some form of bathing was always

popular in Oriental cultures, the Japanese cultivated it into an esthetic experience. Originally, they were known to take tubless baths, with servants pouring water from jugs over the bodies. Later, they took to constructing rather large wooden tubs to set in their courtyards or gardens. These were filled with exceedingly hot water, and the whole family piled in for a bath in one sitting. Hotels offered the same type of bath, either indoors or out, with a massage thrown in for guests. To this day, there is public mixed bathing, with no attempt to achieve privacy. Frequently, public baths have large, unprotected openings through which passersby may view the scene.

Not only does the typographer have to make a decision about the correct style of a typeface, but also about the correct weight and tonal color. In this chapter we'll look into the effect that the right — and wrong — choices of typeface, and in particular spacing, have over the tonal color of various styles of body setting. I'll be illustrating just how you can alter the tonal color of any typeface by simply varying the letter, line and word spacing. I'll also demonstrate the importance of line length and the differences that light, medium, bold and italic variations have on the same copy.

First let me explain what I mean by tonal color. The rather lovely piece of design work shown left appeared in the June 83 edition of *U&l.c.*, the *International Typeface Corporation's* journal. It is set in *Souvenir Light Italic, Souvenir Demi Italic* and *Serif Gothic Heavy*. You can see how the weight of the body copy recedes just enough to allow the illustration to be the focal point, but at the same time loses none of its readability. Note also how the use of italic in the body copy creates a subtle contrast with the strong vertical stress of the illustration and headline, and also with the prominence of the headline. You would normally expect a headline to appear at the head of the design. Here, however, we have an example where the rules have been broken, but broken with understanding and skill. The designer has moved away from the conventional approach to layout, but has still obeyed the basic design priorities, ie.

Priority 1. Headline: The attention-grabber.

Priority 2. Illustration: The means of developing interest.

Priority 3. Copy: The message.

Now let us see how the wrong choice of type weight and spacing can alter the design completely (right). I will repeat the design but this time changing the weights of the typeface. The headline, which was originally set in *Serif Gothic Heavy,* is now set in *Serif Gothic.* I've changed the body copy of the first paragraph from *Souvenir Demi Italic* to *Souvenir Light* and the main body copy from *Souvenir Light Italic* to *Souvenir Bold.* Because the bold type of the body copy now takes more space I've had to reduce its size so that it fits the same area as the original. The leading (the amount of space between the lines) has remained constant to make the design as close to the original as possible.

While I'll admit that my modifications have been a bit extreme, they do prove a point. Gone is the logical sequence of priorities, the headline no longer has an initial impact and the strength of the body copy competes with the illustration for attention. When you look at the body copy you will find that it is far too small in its bold style to be read with comfort.

LETTER SPACING

Tonal color is affected not only by the weight of the typeface but also by its letter spacing, inter-word spacing and line spacing. To a lesser extent it is influenced by the length of line, although this will affect general readability more than tonal color.

First let us look at letter spacing. As you would expect, the term refers to the amount of space between individual characters. Now that we have moved into the computer age out of the era of hot metal setting, in which there were no possibilities at all of close spacing and individual kerning (the

It really isn't sporting to puncture anyone's balloon, but when we read in a trade magazine that, last year alone, Americans spent $2.5 billion on bathrooms and bath-related facilities, we could only think, "Peanuts!" Compared with the attention some of our ancient antecedents paid to bathing and bath facilities, our recent expenditures for, and preoccupation with, bathrooms is just a drip in the tub.

Ancient baths. Five thousand years ago, a highly civilized society dwelling in the Indus Valley had sophisticated bathing equipment — a public bath that measured 24 × 40 feet, with a scientific drainage system, and private bathrooms in their homes with tubs, drains, spigots and faucets.

In the well-preserved palaces of Aegean civilizations, there are recognizable remnants of bathrooms with tubs, footbaths, drains and vertical pipes, proving that, as far back as 2,000 B.C., people were bathing with running water.

Ancient Sumerians, too, were known to have had bathing facilities. But it was Mosaic Law, found in the Bible in Leviticus (16, 17) and Number (19), that first firmly associated washing and bathing with religious duty. Dozens of ritual washings are spelled out in the Bible. Among the more

Some did it for cleanliness. Some did it for Godliness. Some did it for sport. Some did it for pleasure. For one reason or another, for 5,000 years, civilized people have been "turned on" to

ILLUSTRATION BY GINI SHURTLEFF

bathtubs

common practices among orthodox Jews are the required hand-washing before meals and the ritual bath for women, the *mikvah,* before marriage and following menses. There is no mention of required baths for menfolk, but who says life is fair?

The Greeks. The Greeks of ancient times needed no motivation for bathing except for sheer pleasure. They frolicked in tubs of polished stone, marble or wood — first in cold water, then in warm. Bathing, for them, was a purely social and recreational activity in

esthetic surroundings.

Orientals. Although some form of bathing was cultivated it into an esthetic experience. Originally, they were known to take tubless baths, with servants pouring water from jugs over the bodies. Hotels offered the same type of bath, either indoors or out, with a massage thrown in for guests. To this day, there is public mixed bathing, with no attempt to achieve privacy. Frequently, public baths have large, unprotected openings through which passersby may view the scene.

closing up of bad letter combinations such as To, Ye, etc.), we have total control over all forms of spacing. This has meant that many agencies and studios today can adapt their own "house style."

By adjusting letter spacing we can improve legibility appropriate to the particular job.

I will now show you how, by varying the letter spacing, legibility is improved or decreased. This example is set in 12/13pt *Caxton Light* with standard letter spacing.

Set-Size

To understand letter spacing it is important to understand the principles of setting letters. The *unit* is the means by which the width of individual characters (including spaces) is calculated, which relates directly to the *em*.

The *em* is a typographic measurement equal to the square of its particular point size. (It is not to be confused with *pica em*, which is the equivalent of 12 pts.) Therefore a 24pt em is a 24pt square, a 36pt em is a 36pt square, etc.

By dividing the *em* into equal vertical segments you arrive at the *unit*. The number of *units* per *em* varies from system to system, but 18, 32, 36, 48, 54, and 65 are all common, with the latest typesetting machines producing an even greater number of *units* per *em*. It must be appreciated that the *unit* is a proportional measurement. For example, with a 54 *unit* system, a single *unit* will represent 1/54 of the type size, whether it is 12pt, 36pt or 48pt.

The way the system works is that each character is allocated a certain number of *units*. This dimension is referred to as the character's *set-width* or *set-size*, and includes a small amount of space to either side of the character to prevent characters from touching when they are set. The *set width* of a particular character will obviously vary from typeface to typeface, to take into account the variations within the various faces and the differenes between medium, condensed and expanded, etc. It is by adding to, or subtracting from, the *set width* of the characters that variations in letter spacing can be achieved, either by collective or individual adjustment.

Fashions come and go. This certainly applies very much to typographical design, and in particular, to letter spacing. When computer-generated setting first arrived and the advantages of its infinitely flexible letter spacing were recognized, very tight letter spacing, particularly for headlines, soon became fashionable. Now, however, the movement is in the opposite direction, with many designers opting for an extremely open style of typography reminiscent of the 1950s. This control over letter spacing means that you can alter the tonal color of your body copy subtly by varying the standard spacing. This is done by adding, or subtracting, units from the set width. But all designers must remember that, when all is said and done, we are communicators. Our messages have to be read and understood. Letters that are too close or too open, designed for the sake of fashion at the expense of legibility, do NOT make good typography.

12/13pt Caxton Light (standard letter spacing)

I will now repeat the previous passage, but this time reducing the set width from its standard setting to –1 of the standard.

The previous style works well and is popular for advertising setting, especially with serif typefaces. It does not always work so well with condensed sans serif faces because the vertical stress becomes too strong, as the following short paragraph illustrates. It is set in *Univers Medium Condensed* , –1.

Fashions come and go. This certainly applies very much to typographical design, and in particular, to letter spacing. When computer-generated setting first arrived and the advantages of its infinitely flexible letter spacing were recognized, very tight letter spacing, particularly for headlines, soon became fashionable. Now, however, the movement is in the opposite direction, with many designers opting for an extremely open style of typography reminiscent of the 1950s. This control over letter spacing means that you can alter the tonal color of your body copy subtly by varying the standard spacing. This is done by adding, or subtracting, units from the set width. But all designers must remember that, when all is said and done, we are communicators. Our messages have to be read and understood. Letters that are too close or too open, designed for the sake of fashion at the expense of legibility, do NOT make good typography.

12/13pt Caxton Light (-1 letter spacing)

Fashions come and go. This certainly applies very much to typographical design, and in particular, to letter spacing. When computer-generated setting first arrived and the advantages of its infinitely flexible letter spacing were recognized, very tight letter spacing, particularly for headlines, soon became fashionable. Now, however, the movement is in the opposite direction, with many designers opting for an extremely open style of typography reminiscent of the 1950s. This control over letter spacing means that you can alter the tonal color of your body copy subtly by varying the standard spacing. This is done by adding, or subtracting, units from the set width. But all designers must remember that, when all is said and done, we are communicators. Our messages have to be read and understood. Letters that are too close or too open, designed for the sake of fashion at the expense of legibility, do NOT make good typography.

12/13pt Univers Medium Condensed (-1 letter spacing)

Now look back to the example in *Caxton Light* and compare it with this piece, which shows what happens when space is over-reduced and legibility sacrificed. The set width is now reduced to -5. The individual characters are now "kissing," creating a rather unpleasant style of setting.

Fashions come and go. This certainly applies very much to typographical design, and in particular, to letter spacing. When computer-generated setting first arrived and the advantages of its infinitely flexible letter spacing were recognized, very tight letter spacing, particularly for headlines, soon became fashionable. Now, however, the movement is in the opposite direction, with many designers opting for an extremely open style of typography reminiscent of the 1950s. This control over letter spacing means that you can alter the tonal color of your body copy subtly by varying the standard spacing. This is done by adding, or subtracting, units from the set width. But all designers must remember that, when all is said and done, we are communicators. Our messages have to be read and understood. Letters that are too close or too open, designed for the sake of fashion at the expense of legibility, do NOT make good typography.

12/13pt Caxton Light (-5 letter spacing)

We can, on the other hand, move the other way on the setting scale and increase the set width. This example represents +1 spacing.

Fashions come and go. This certainly applies very much to typographical design, and in particular, to letter spacing. When computer-generated setting first arrived and the advantages of its infinitely flexible letter spacing were recognized, very tight letter spacing, particularly for headlines, soon became fashionable. Now, however, the movement is in the opposite direction, with many designers opting for an extremely open style of typography reminiscent of the 1950s. This control over letter spacing means that you can alter the tonal color of your body copy subtly by varying the standard spacing. This is done by adding, or subtracting, units from the set width. But all designers must remember that, when all is said and done, we are communicators. Our messages have to be read and understood. Letters that are too close or too open, designed for the sake of fashion at the expense of legibility, do NOT make good typography.

12/13pt Caxton Light (+1 letter spacing)

Extra spacing can work well but, as with reduced spacing, it can be overdone. Setting the letters to +5, for example, as shown below, creates an unpleasant effect. This example does not read well because of the openness of the letter spacing compared to the closeness of the line spacing.

Fashions come and go. This certainly applies very much to typographical design, and in particular, to letter spacing. When computer-generated setting first arrived and the advantages of its infinitely flexible letter spacing were recognized, very tight letter spacing, particularly for head-lines, soon became fashionable. Now, however, the movement is in the opposite direction, with many designers opting for an extremely open style of typography reminiscent of the 1950s. This control over letter spacing means that you can alter the tonal color of your body copy subtly by varying the standard spacing. This is done by adding, or subtracting, units from the set width. But all designers must remember that, when all is said and done, we are communicators. Our messages have to be read and understood. Letters that are too close or too open, designed for the sake of fashion at the expense of legibility, do NOT make good typography.

12/13pt Caxton Light (+5 letter spacing)

But look what happens when I open up the line spacing from 12/13pt to 12/16pt.

Fashions come and go. This certainly applies very much to typographical design, and in particular, to letter spacing. When computer-generated setting first arrived and the advantages of its infinitely flexible letter spacing were recognized, very tight letter spacing, particularly for head-lines, soon became fashionable. Now, however, the movement is in the opposite direction, with many designers opting for an extremely open style of typography reminiscent of the 1950s. This control over letter spacing means that you can alter the tonal color of your body copy subtly by varying the standard spacing. This is done by adding, or subtracting, units from the set width. But all designers must remember that, when all is said and done, we are communicators. Our messages have to be read and understood. Letters that are too close or too open, designed for the sake of fashion at the expense of legibility, do NOT make good typography.

12/16pt Caxton Light (+5 letter spacing)

Word spacing can also be controlled, but again too much or too little space can affect legibility. Used with care it can provide your work with just the amount of tonal variation that you are seeking.

As you would expect, word spacing is affected by the style of typeface chosen. Condensed faces require less space than expanded faces do, and small type sizes read better with a little extra word spacing. I find that, as a general guide, the ideal word space represents 2/3 the width of the lower case "o," but this is only a starting point.

The unit system is used on computer typesetting machines for measuring the width of each type character and for calculating overall width and counting. It's a simple system based on the square of any given size of type, commonly known as the em. Each em is divided into a given number of units. These can vary from typesetting system to system machine, but the division of 54 units to the em is not uncommon. Each character will be allocated to a given number of units which decide the width of each character. The size of the typeface does not affect the number of allocated units, ie. a capital M in Times Roman could be allocated 54 units. This allocation of 54 unit divisions would apply whether the size were to be in 10pt, 24pt or 48pt. The diagram illustrates how the divisions are allocated. Note how each character is allocated additional spacing both to its left and right. This

18 units

Right A self-promotional piece of typography by New Yorker, Robert Wakeman. The principal typeface, used to good effect, is ITC Galliard. The hung initials for each paragraph over a two-line depth is a nice touch, together with his use of Bold and Italic within the text to illustrate specific points. Notice too the inter-character spacing of the headline. It is a very tight style that has allowed certain characters to touch, thus avoiding too much white space between the awkward character combinations.

Look at the space in, and around, and in between the letters above. This is called the negative space. But good negative space does not come about simply by spacing out each letter equally, or by doing so mechanically. This creates irregular space between letters. The negative space must be given some uniformity of visual weight around the letter, in order to be balanced and pleasing to the eye.

Good designers and typographers gain, over the years, experience in knowing how much negative space to put between each two letters. This means more than just putting letters next to each other. Capital letters are more difficult to do than the lowercase letters. The same holds true for the thinner weights. The larger the letter, the more important the negative space. The negative spaces between the serif typefaces are more graceful and easier to accomplish, design-wise, than the sans-serif typefaces. The latter almost require the skill at geometry of an architect.

Certain fundamental principles should be taken into consideration when dealing with negative spaces. Letter combinations that have almost no space at all between them. Vertical stroke against vertical stroke. This includes such combinations as **AW, AV, IM, IN, II,** etc. These are often put too close together, especially when setting sans-serif typefaces. The trained eye will allow enough space in such combinations to complement the other letters in the word.

Again, there are certain letter combinations with unavoidably large negative spaces. For example, **LA, TT, IT, TY, LL, LE,** and the like. They can be overlapped slightly, or altered, to cut down on the negative space between letters, and the rest of the word can be spaced out visually to please the eye. This does not mean, however, that all other letters in that word are to have the same amount of space between them as the examples above. But one has to take into consideration the space inside and around each letter to get the proper negative space. *(The combinations would be verticals next to curves; curves next to curves; and open curves next to verticals.)*

Today's great type designers are masters at what they do. They spend hours creating masterpieces out of letters of the alphabet. Each letter must have its uniqueness, but not be too expressive, so as to overpower the other letters in the alphabet. There should be a good relationship between the upper and lowercase characters as well. The type designer is also concerned with the balance of the black positive areas of each letter, and how to capture harmonious whites *(negative space)* inside the letters, as well as between them.

One well-known designer and art director in the New York City area always looks at the negative space first, before looking at the positive areas.

So, when taking all of the above into consideration, the creative person can enhance the beauty of the typeface design by the proper use of the negative space. The result? Typographical masterpieces!

presents the individual characters from touching during the setting process. It is possible to reduce or increase the spacing between the various characters either collectively or individually (a process known as kerning) by programing the computer to either reduce or increase the number of set units allocated to each individual character.

Here are a few examples. The following text has been set with standard word spacing, flush left, in 10/11 pt *ITC New Baskerville.*

Too much or too little space between words can seriously affect legibility. Too little space can cause the individual words to merge as one, creating difficulties for the reader in distinguishing one word from another; too much space can cause rivers that disrupt the natural movement of the eye from left to right. Rivers are a common problem within narrow measure justification.

Now here is the same example, but with tight word spacing:

Too much or too little space between words can seriously affect legibility. Too little space can cause the individual words to merge as one, creating difficulties for the reader in distinguishing one word from another; too much space can cause rivers that disrupt the natural movement of the eye from left to right. Rivers are a common problem within narrow measure justification.

And this time the example has been given very open word spacing:

Too much or too little space between words can seriously affect legibility. Too little space can cause the individual words to merge as one, creating difficulties for the reader in distinguishing one word from another; too much space can cause rivers that disrupt the natural movement of the eye from left to right. Rivers are a common problem within narrow measure justification.

Left It isn't only body copy that can create gray tones, the same effects can be achieved by spacing condensed caps closely, as this poster for "New ideas for design" clearly illustrates. I like the way the red blocks of color have been used as a means of giving the text full justification without exaggerated word spacing. The design was by Grundy & Northedge.

This next example **(1)** is justified within a fairly narrow measure. This is when the problems of excessive rivers occur. It is a typical problem experienced with newspaper typography. ("River" is the term given to large areas of white space that run down through the text, caused by excessive word spacing.)

While the legibility of this example is the norm in newsprint, it is totally unacceptable for work that requires quality setting. But how do you improve the word spacing within the restrictions of the justified, narrow measure? The obvious answer is hyphenation. By the introduction of just two hyphens you can create an entirely new feel in the paragraph. Note how the hyphens are hung in the margin, in the example below **(2)**. Although they go beyond the measure, the effect of the hung punctuation creates a more even righthand edge. In the previous example the punctuation was set within the measure. Although this example is considerably improved by the addition of hyphenation, there are still one or two lines that contain excessive word spacing.

This unsatisfactory visual problem can by improved by the introduction of semi-justification **(3)**. This style is popular with advertising agencies. It requires all lines that fall beyond a predetermined point within the measure to be justified, whereas those that fall naturally short of the specified point fall unjustified.

1 Too much or too little space between words can seriously affect legibility. Too little space can cause the individual words to merge as one, creating difficulties for the reader in distinguishing one word from another; too much space can cause rivers that disrupt the natural movement of the eye from left to right. Rivers are a common problem within narrow measure justification.

2 Too much or too little space between words can seriously affect legibility. Too little space can cause the individual words to merge as one, creating difficulties for the reader in distinguishing one word from another; too much space can cause rivers that disrupt the natural movement of the eye from left to right. Rivers are a common problem within narrow measure justification.

3 Too much or too little space between words can seriously affect the legibility. Too little space can cause the individual words to merge as one, creating difficulties for the reader in distinguishing one word from another; too much space can cause rivers that disrupt the natural movement of the eye from left to right. Rivers are a common problem within narrow measure justification.

4 Too much or too little space between words can seriously affect legibility. Too little space can cause the individual words to merge as one, creating difficulties for the reader in distinguishing one word from another; too much space can cause rivers that disrupt the natural movement of the eye from left to right. Rivers are a common problem within narrow measure justification.

Semi-justification was devised by two British typographers, David Kelsey and Ed Everley, when they were working for an advertising agency called Cogent Elliott. They therefore named their new system Cogent left. Now slightly modified, the system is still often called Cogent left in Britain, although the term semi-justification is becoming widely used there, as well as in the U.S.

You saw in the first example how short line lengths could create excessive word spacing and consequently affect legibility. Extra long measures can also hinder readability and understanding. The ideal number of characters per line for body copy is around the 36 to 50 mark. When the number of characters goes well beyond that point, to 80 and above (**4**), readability suffers considerably.

At The Villages of Fernbrook, lunch with the family can be a real picnic.

Our lifestyle just naturally seems to bring families closer together. The picnic area is a great place for family fun. The kids will love playing in the shade of tall trees and exploring wooded trails. There's even a pond for romantic strolls, skipping stones or just daydreaming.

So come visit our two, three and four bedroom colonial-style homes today. The Villages of Fernbrook include Chatham Grove, Taylor's Landing I and II, Olde Williamsburg and Old Fernbrook. There's even special financing available that makes these homes very affordable.

You'll find plenty of room for growing families and you'll discover life here can be a real picnic.

Models open from 1 p.m. til dusk. Go west 3 miles on Rt. 360 from Chippenham, left on Fordham Rd. Follow the signs.

Equal Housing Opportunity

VILLAGES OF Fernbrook

15

WHY IT TAKES 15 TYPESETTING OPERATIONS TO INSERT JUST ONE LITTLE WORD OF COPY IN YOUR AD. **1.** THE CHANGE IS PHONED IN. **2.** IT'S ENTERED ON A TIME SHEET AND JOB TICKET. **3.** THEN IT'S SENT TO THE COMPOSING ROOM. **4.** THE OPERATOR INTERRUPTS THE JOB ON WHICH HE'S WORKING. **5.** HE MAKES A VARIETY OF MACHINE ADJUSTMENTS AND BRINGS THE ORIGINAL SETTING UP ONTO THE SCREEN. **6.** HE INSERTS THE NEW WORD INTO THE PARAGRAPH AND SETS A SLUG LINE FOR IDENTIFICATION. **7.** THE CORRECTED COPY IS THEN RUN OUT. **8.** THE EXPOSED FILM IS DEVELOPED, FIXED, WASHED, AND DRIED IN A SEPARATE AUTOMATIC PROCESSOR. **9.** THE CORRECTED COPY IS THEN SENT TO A STRIPPER, WHO MUST LOCATE THE ORIGINAL FILM MECHANICAL TO BE ADJUSTED. **10.** HE FINDS THE FILM MECHANICAL AND PLACES IT ON HIS LIGHT TABLE, INSERTS THE CORRECTION AND SENDS THE FORM TO THE PROOFING DEPARTMENT. **11.** THE FILM IS PROOFED ONCE, AND THEN SENT TO A READER TO CHECK THE CORRECTNESS OF THE NEW COPY. **12.** THEN BACK TO THE PROOFING DEPARTMENT, WHERE THE CORRECT NUMBER OF REVISED PROOFS ARE PULLED. **13.** THE FILM MECHANICAL IS RETURNED TO ITS ORIGINAL AND CORRECT LOCATION IN STORAGE. **14.** TIME RECORDS FOR BILLING PURPOSES ARE ENTERED. **15.** THE REVISED PROOFS ARE SENT BY MESSENGER TO THE AGENCY.

Despite the importance of letter and word spacing, the biggest single factor that will affect the tonal gray of the body copy is line spacing. Light type can look strong and medium copy weak just by a varia-

tion of the leading. These next examples alter the value of the copy as they progress from –1pt leading through +4pt leading. The examples are set in 9pt *Parlament Roman.*

Just as word and letter spacing affect the tonal grays of your body copy, so will the space between each line affect its legibility and tonal color. The choice of typeface, type size, and line length are other factors to consider, but line spacing decisions are usually made around the correct tonal color for the design problem rather than being restricted by the norm for the chosen typeface.

-1pt leading (9/8pt)

Just as word and letter spacing affect the tonal grays of your body copy, so will the space between each line affect its legibility and tonal color. The choice of typeface, type size, and line length are other factors to consider, but line spacing decisions are usually made around the correct tonal color for the design problem rather than being restricted by the norm for the chosen typeface.

+1pt leading (9/10pt)

Just as word and letter spacing affect the tonal grays of your body copy, so will the space between each line affect its legibility and tonal color. The choice of typeface, type size, and line length are other factors to consider, but line spacing decisions are usually made around the correct tonal color for the design problem rather than being restricted by the norm for the chosen typeface.

+3pt leading (9/12pt)

Just as word and letter spacing affect the tonal grays of your body copy, so will the space between each line affect its legibility and tonal color. The choice of typeface, type size, and line length are other factors to consider, but line spacing decisions are usually made around the correct tonal color for the design problem rather than being restricted by the norm for the chosen typeface.

set solid (9/9pt)

Just as word and letter spacing affect the tonal grays of your body copy, so will the space between each line affect its legibility and tonal color. The choice of typeface, type size, and line length are other factors to consider, but line spacing decisions are usually made around the correct tonal color for the design problem rather than being restricted by the norm for the chosen typeface.

+2 pt (9/11pt)

Just as word and letter spacing affect the tonal grays of your body copy, so will the space between each line affect its legibility and tonal color. The choice of typeface, type size, and line length are other factors to consider, but line spacing decisions are usually made around the correct tonal color for the design problem rather than being restricted by the norm for the chosen typeface.

+4pt (9/13pt)

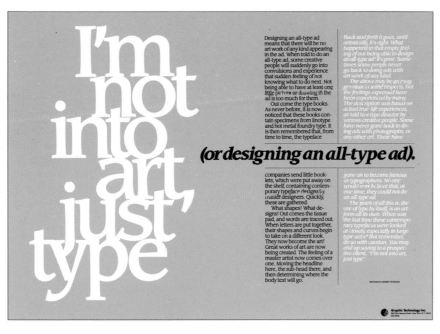

I'm not into art, just type

(or designing an all-type ad).

Designing an all-type ad means that there will be no art work of any kind appearing in the ad. When told to do an all-type ad, some creative people will suddenly go into convulsions and experience that sudden feeling of not knowing what to do next. Not being able to have at least one little picture or drawing in the ad is too much for them.

Out come the type books. As never before, it is now noticed that these books contain specimens from linotype and hot metal foundry type. It is then remembered that, from time to time, the typeface companies send little booklets, which were put away on the shelf, containing contemporary typeface designs by master designers. Quickly, these are gathered.

What shapes! What designs! Out comes the tissue pad, and words are traced out. When letters are put together, their shapes and curves begin to take on a different look. They now become the art! Great works of art are now being created. The feeling of a master artist now comes over one. Moving the headline here, the sub-head there, and then determining where the body text will go.

Back and forth it goes, until artistically, it's right. What happened to that empty feeling of not being able to design an all-type ad? It's gone. Sometimes some people never go back to doing ads with art work of any kind.

The above may be an exaggeration in some respects, but the feelings expressed have been experienced by many. The description was based on actual true-life experiences, as told to a type director by various creative people. Some have never gone back to doing ads with photographs, or any other art. These have gone on to become famous as typographers. No one would ever believe that, at one time, they could not do an all-type ad.

The point of all this is: the use of type by itself, is an art form all its own. When was the last time these contemporary typefaces were looked at closely, especially in large type sizes? But remember, do so with caution. You may end up saying to a prospective client, "I'm not into art, just type."

DESIGNED BY ROBERT WAKEMAN

Graphic Technology Inc.

DESIGN EXPERTISE 1985

Dale Chihuly

"We discovered the technique for our cylinders in the summer of 1974 at Pilchuck, our farm north of Seattle, and I remember how thrilled we were to find we could lay out a drawing with bits of glass which, when we came down on it with molten glass, would fuse and mold together as it was blown out. I began a series of cylinders to further explore the idea of drawing into glass. I go back to the series now and then because the process is still unpredictable and continues to stimulate me.

"I saw some Northwest Coast Indian blankets in the Tacoma Historical Society and thought I would try blowing some very thin basketlike forms which would appear crumpling and collapsing under their own weight. I didn't want them symmetrical. It was quite a discovery to see what I could do with just air, fire and gravity using hardly any tools. In the summer of 1977, I made about 100 baskets, all the same color (tabak), and they were shown on a steel table at the Seattle Art Museum.

"At one point, I went to Murano to study. Strange, I and others are still carrying on the Venetian tradition. They're losing it over there because of modern technology. There doesn't seem to be the desire for handmade glasses when glasses made by machines are available at less cost. People would rather drive a Porsche, which is made by machine, than a more expensive Rolls-Royce, which is primarily made by hand.

"We start blowing at 4 a.m. and work straight through with no breaks. The blowing just seems to go better on the early schedule. It's quieter and the shop is cooler and the glass is at its best in the morning. I don't know why. And we have more privacy. We then stop for a big lunch — lots of Italian fare. This has a pull on my social life. Maybe that's why I never got married.

The last few years I've been a kind of nomad, working with my traveling team in many different universities and shops around the United States and in Europe.

"When I'm not traveling for my work, I'm often traveling for pleasure. Every year or two, I visit some unusual archipelago of islands — most recently the Orkneys and the Scilly Islands off Great Britain and the coast of Brittany. I love islands. I'm fascinated by the fact that, being isolated, they develop uniquely."

Above left The example by Robert Wakeman, with its subheading running through the text, uses discretionary hyphenation to prevent lines of too short a measure. **Above** This piece is not primarily text setting, but is a good design example of headlines and subheads set flush right. **Left** The designers, Bennett Robinson and Paula Zographos, have avoided both hyphenation and lines of short measure probably by means of intelligent copy editing.

Ultimately, tonal grays are determined by the typeface you use. Look at the comparison of different typefaces using the same copy (shown on these pages). All are set to the same measure (16½ ems), size and leading (10/11 pt) and depth (11 lines), and yet the tonal grays are quite different.

Century Schoolbook

Excellence in typography is the result of nothing more than an attitude. Its appeal comes from the understanding used in its planning; the designer must care. In contemporary advertising the perfect integration of design elements often demands unorthodox typography. It may require the use of compact spacing, minus leading, unusual sizes and weights; whatever is needed to improve appearance and impact. Stating specific principles or guides on the subject of typography is difficul

Fenice Bold

Excellence in typography is the result of nothing more than an attitude. Its appeal comes from the understanding used in its planning; the designer must care. In contemporary advertising the perfect integration of design elements often demands unorthodox typography. It may require the use of compact spacing, minus leading, unusual sizes and weights; whatever is needed to improve appearance and impact. Stating specific principles or guides on the subject of typography is d

Gill Sans Extra Bold

Excellence in typography is the result of nothing more than an attitude. Its appeal comes from the understanding used in its planning; the designer must care. In contemporary advertising the perfect integration of design elements often demands unorthodox typography. It may require the use of compact spacing, minus leading, unusual sizes and weights; whatever is needed to improve appearance and impact. Stating specific principles o

Goudy Old Style Roman

Excellence in typography is the result of nothing more than an attitude. Its appeal comes from the understanding used in its planning; the designer must care. In contemporary advertising the perfect integration of design elements often demands unorthodox typography. It may require the use of compact spacing, minus leading, unusual sizes and weights; whatever is needed to improve appearance and impact. Stating specific principles or guides on the subject of typography is difficult because the principle applying to one job may not fit the next. N

Medieval Italic

Excellence in typography is the result of nothing more than an attitude. Its appeal comes from the understanding used in its planning; the designer must care. In contemporary advertising the perfect integration of design elements often demands unorthodox typography. It may require the use of compact spacing, minus leading, unusual sizes and weights; whatever is needed to improve appearance and impact. Stating specific principles or guides on the subject of typography is difficult because the principle applying to one job may not fit the

Rockwell Roman

Excellence in typography is the result of nothi ng more than an attitude. Its appeal comes fro m the understanding used in its planning; the designer must care. In contemporary advertis ing the perfect integration of design element s often demands unorthodox typography. It m ay require the use of compact spacing, minus leading, unusual sizes and weights; whatever i s needed to improve appearance and impact . Stating specific principles or guides on the s ubject of typography is difficult because the p

Univers 45 Light

Excellence in typography is the result of nothin g more than an attitude. Its appeal comes fro m the understanding used in its planning; the designer must care. In contemporary adverti sing the perfect integration of design elements often demands unorthodox typography. It ma y require the use of compact spacing, minus le ading, unusual sizes and weights; whatever is needed to improve appearance and impact. St ating specific principles or guides on the subje ct of typography is difficult because the princip

Typecolor

The copy has been written, the artwork is finished, the layout has taken shape, the headline typeface has been chosen. Now for the body text. In addition to the type-face that will be chosen, what color will it be? Color?

You could choose to have it printed in any color imaginable to go with the design. In fact, there's been a trend for printing the text in one color, with the sentences that are to stand out printed in another color, and it can look great.

But the color referred to at the outset is the type that is to be printed in black.

Generally, today's typefaces released from the noted typeface companies are released in four or five different weights. Light, book, medium, bold and black. In type specimen books, there are blocks of body text settings in these various weights. A good type specimen book will show the typefaces set solid, and with added leading (*extra space between the lines*). This can have an effect on the color.

When looking at these blocks of text, one begins to see various shades of grey, ranging from very light grey to almost solid black. The shade of grey will depend upon the design of the typeface.

Now, getting back to the question, which color will you choose?

Designers and art directors who are concerned about the typecolor have various reasons for choosing different weights of body text.

One way which has been used with good success is the different percentage values found in a screen tint scale. This works best when it is on a clear piece of film.

Lay this next to the artwork, headline type, or photographs (*color, or black & white halftones*), and see what shade works best. Then find in the type specimen book the typeface to be used, and choose the weight that matches the screen value that looked the best.

When using this method, it has often been found that the darker weights of the body text look better with line drawings and lighter halftones. (*Light line drawings get lost next to very thin lightweight body text.*) On the other hand, lighter body text looks best next to darker artwork, and halftones.

Those who design magazine formats generally use a medium weight typeface for the body text, because they deal with all kinds of artwork and photographs.

The secret is to get viewers so involved in reading the material and enjoying the layouts that they don't mind the pieces being in black and white. This, of course, is important when the budget does not allow for color. Color?

The body text. What color will it be?

Left This example by typographer Robert Wakeman is similar in style to his previous designs, set flush left and ragged right and with much the same use of discretionary hyphenation. The headline spacing is tight, and again he's not afraid to allow certain characters to "kiss." This example illustrates very well the pleasing use of hanging indentation as an alternative style to standard paragraph indentation. The typefaces used are ITC Novarese bold italic and ITC Berkeley Old Style.

Below This is a wonderful example of the marriage between photography, design, typography and white space. Simha Fordsham, Jonas Tse and Nancy Leung of Olympia & York Developments Ltd all had a hand in this design for 425 Lexington Avenue, New York. The prominent typographical feature is the ultra-condensed cap A (in Empire) which covers a depth of eight lines into the Century Old Style body type. It breaks up what could otherwise have been an ordinary block of text.

VARIATION FOR EMPHASIS

All the previous examples are ways in which the designer can create tonal variety and impact with the body copy. But there are many occasions, especially in advertising, when tonal variety is needed to lay a particular emphasis or accent. This emphasis is created easily by the intelligent inclusion of italics, capital letters, underscoring, additional faces from the chosen type family, or other contrasting typefaces compatible with the main body copy.

When deciding which words, phrases, etc. need to stand out, and to what degree, remember that too much emphasis can have the opposite effect to the one you want. Overlong phrases can lose their punch if the reader loses track of where the extra stress is intended. The amount of copy and where it occurs within the main body of text will also influ-ence its emphasis. A single word in the middle of a large section of body copy can easily be lost with the wrong treatment, and will need to be high-lighted differently from a word that is emphasized at the beginning of a paragraph.

The use of *italic* is a simple method of drawing attention to a single word or short phrase. It is an easy way to highlight the occasional word *without* altering the tonal color of the body copy.

If the copy requires some extra emphasis it can be achieved by the introduction of CAPITAL LET-TERS, but they can sometimes alter balance and readability if a phrase or sentence is too long to be taken in at one glance.

On the other hand the introduction of SMALL CAPS can offer a different alternative to the more aggressive full-sized capital. Their use is ideal for letterheads in which directors have lengthy *qualif-*

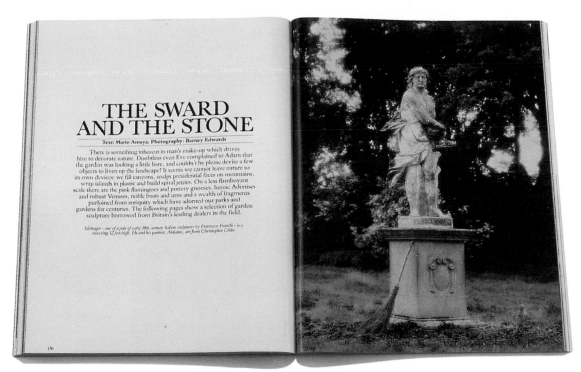

THE SWARD AND THE STONE

Text: Mario Amaya. Photography: Barney Edwards

There is something inherent in man's make-up which drives him to decorate nature. Doubtless even Eve complained to Adam that the garden was looking a little bare, and couldn't he please devise a few objects to liven up the landscape? It seems we cannot leave nature to its own devices; we fill canyons, sculpt presidential faces on mountains, wrap islands in plastic and build spiral jetties. On a less flamboyant scale there are the pink flamingoes and pottery gnomes, heroic Adonises and robust Venuses, noble busts and urns and a wealth of fragments purloined from antiquity which have adorned our parks and gardens for centuries. The following pages show a selection of garden sculpture borrowed from Britain's leading dealers in the field.

Meleager - one of a pair of early 18th century Italian sculptures by Francesco Franchi - is a towering 12 feet high. He and his partner, Atalanta, are from Christopher Gibbs.

136

ications. When ordering small caps make sure that your typesetter has a true, small caps font and doesn't try to get away with a smaller point size of your chosen typeface. There is a difference.

Probably the most common method of emphasizing text is by increasing the weight of your typeface, from light to medium, or medium to bold. It attracts attention and is hard to ignore. Unlike italic, caps and small caps, **it will have a greater effect upon the tonal balance of your layout.** This is usually the very reason for using the heavier weight of type.

The introduction of a different typeface within the body copy to make a point needs far more control. The reason for the change has to be sound. Unless it is used for subheadings, titles, or captions, it rarely works. Where it does work, and with very good effect, is in magazines and illustrated books.

There are other means of creating color variation within your designs and we'll look at these as we progress through the book.

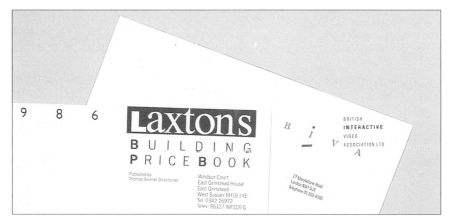

Right This design, by Robert Wakeman, is a very good example of type variation and how it can create tonal contrast. He has combined italic and bold italic, using the bold for the first line of each paragraph, and has then reversed this image with bold and light Roman, using the light face to start each paragraph. It is not immediately obvious but he has also varied the weights of his headline. Each line was set in the same face but in a different weight and size. The boxed headline shows what it would have looked like if the three weights were set in the same size.

That's a loaded question. It's like asking an interior designer 'How should I decorate my apartment?' Would the designer reply instantly or rather wisely begin asking such questions as: What kind of style do you like? What kind of mood do you want to create? Do you want all rooms to follow a particular theme, or do you want each room to be different? After getting some answers to such questions, the designer can begin to start giving some suggestions, and perhaps show some samples of what is being recommended and why **Is it really any** *different when someone bursts into a type director's office and cries out, 'Quick! A typeface. What do you recommend?'*

Sometimes it is presumed that type directors can and should be able to recommend a particular typeface at the drop of a hat, and if they can't do so, they're not doing their job right. But that's not true any more than that the interior designer can advise you on how to decorate your apartment without asking some initial questions first. **Some of the** *questions that might be asked when determining what typeface should be used for a particular project are: Who is the client? What is the product? What kind of mood do you want to create? Is there any artwork, or is it an all-type ad? What is the headline copy? What does the layout look like? How much body text is there?* **As the type** *director begins to get answers to such questions, then some recommendations can be made, and samples shown. Equally important are the reasons for such recommendations. As the creative person looks at the samples and listens to the reasons, then selections can be made.*

One of the most important parts of an ad is **the headline. Its purpose is to catch the eye of the viewer and attract attention to the subject, drawing a person into the material. For this reason, the selection of the headline typeface should be done with great care.**

There are those who prefer certain rules when **it comes to setting headlines. For example, that all headlines should be set in upper and lower case for a more personal approach and readability. "All caps" say others, for a more forceful message. To follow such rules arbitrarily can limit the designer in the creation of effective and good-looking headlines.**

Today's great type designers are giving us **typefaces that are not only well-designed, but also come in at least four different weights. This is important to the creative person, because what might not work in one weight can work in another weight, and still stay within the same typeface family that you have selected.**

The following are some suggestions that have **proved effective in creating well-designed headlines: First, look at the headline copy. Notice which letters of the alphabet occur most frequently. After deciding what kind of mood you want to create, begin looking at certain typeface styles that will draw attention to your subject. Compare the various letters of the alphabet that will be used in the headline in each typeface family. It won't take long, after this, to decide which typeface to use.**

If you're selecting a headline typeface for a **campaign, of course, you don't know what future headline copy will be. So a great deal will depend upon the kind of mood you want to create for the entire campaign, and whether or not it will look better in all caps or in upper and lower case. Some characters may be altered** *slightly* **to make the typeface customized to make it unique for the client.**

Look at the headline on this poster. How many **weights of this typeface were used? At first glance, it might seem that only one weight was used. But look again. Actually, three weights were used, Mixage book, medium and black. Notice in the box below how these three weights would look if they were all set in the same size.**

Where is it inscribed in stone that all headlines **have to be set in the same weight? By combining the different weights of the same typeface family, effective and attention-getting headlines can be created, and still stay within the framework of good typographic design standards, not the "bubble gum graphics" that look like they belong on the sides of cereal boxes. The idea in selecting different weights of the same typeface family for the headline is to keep each weight to the same thickness throughout. Remember, the typefaces are there, and more are being designed every year. They are just waiting for your recommendations.**

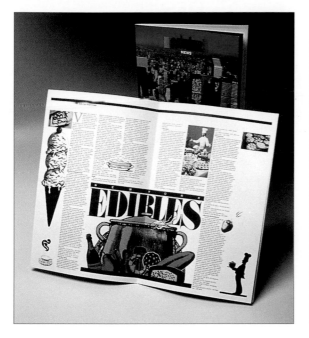

■ **Above left** A very colorful double-page spread designed by Vásken Kalayjian of the Glazer Kalayjian Studio. With the main text set in Times Roman the use of colored illustrations and simple run-arounds has created life and interest in this spread.

■ **Above** A superb double-page spread from Pentagram UK. The typographic information is all there but in no way does it interfere with the beautiful photography. An excellent example of functional layout and typography, it contains no gimmicks, just sensible design.

■ **Left** A Pentagram UK design for the "World" magazine. Work of this nature often has the restrictions of just one or two-color printings. This is one such piece. A great deal of importance has been placed on the creative use of white space.

ave any color you like so long as it's black*"

Has the question ever occurred to you why so much magazine typography, particularly the headlines for advertising copy, appears in black only when the facilities for full color typography are available? The reason can't be the extra cost, because the price of the color separations will already have been met. The reason must therefore be one of readability.

BLACK ON WHITE VERSUS
WHITE ON BLACK

Generally speaking, black type on white is extremely legible; conversely white type reversed out of black is not. White reversed out of black can be visually strong, but only if the right face is used. For example, a fine serif face below 12pt for large areas of text is not a good idea because the words will not be clear. Also, the quality of platemaking, and particularly the inking of the press rollers, must be perfect since there is a strong tendency for the serifs to fill in. If the typeface contains fine hairline strokes, these too can be lost.

Studies have been made concerning the clarity of white type reversed out of black — with startling results. These results showed that for large areas of text, readability was reduced by some 50 percent. The main reason for this is that our eyes suffer strain when we read through large areas of reversed-out type. The degree of reduced comprehension will increase still further if the print quality is poor. Also, when white type is reversed out of a four-color background, as opposed to just

black, further problems will occur if the registration is not perfect. This often occurs with mass-produced magazine work and newsprint in full-color.

These findings should affect your approach to typography and color, because if the visual effect of white out of black, or any other color for that matter, jeopardizes the understanding of the message and the information, then it is not good design.

Sometimes white type is essential to fulfill a particular design requirement. The most successful faces come from the stronger moderns, such as *Souvenir, Congress* and *Bookman.* These faces have little contrast between their thick and thin strokes, and have strong serifs which are less likely to suffer from poor platemaking, registration or printing. Medium or semi-bold sans serifs can also be considered, but their stronger vertical stress needs increased leading to counter it.

* Back in the thirties the Ford Motor Company ran a series of famous advertisements for their Model T Ford which said, "You can have any color you like so long as it's black."

■ The following two pages illustrate different faces reversed out of black in two type sizes, 12/14pt and 6½/8½. Note how the smaller Rockwell reads better than the 12pt Fenice light. Always take extra care when attempting such effects.

Rockwell Regular

Generally speaking, black on white type is extremely legible; conversely white type reversed out of black is not. White reversed out of black can be visually strong, but only if the right face is used. For example, a fine serif face below 12pt for large areas of text is not a good idea because the words will not be clear. Also, the quality of plate-making, and particularly the inking of the press rollers, must be perfect since there is a strong tendency for the serifs to fill in.

Rockwell Regular

Generally speaking, black on white type is extremely legible; conversely white type reversed out of black is not. White reversed out of black can be visually strong, but only if the right face is used. For example, a fine serif face below 12pt for large areas of text is not a good idea because the words will not be clear. Also, the quality of platemaking, and particularly the inking of the press rollers, must be perfect since there is a strong tendency for the serifs to fill in. If the typeface contains fine hairline strokes, these too can be lost.

Gill Sans

Generally speaking, black on white type is extremely legible; conversely white type reversed out of black is not. White reversed out of black can be visually strong, but only if the right face is used. For example, a fine serif face below 12pt for large areas of text is not a good idea because the words will not be clear. Also, the quality of platemaking, and particularly the inking of the press rollers, must be perfect since there is a strong tendency for the serifs to fill in. If the typeface contains fine hairline strokes, these too can be lost.

Gill Sans

Generally speaking, black on white type is extremely legible; conversely white type reversed out of black is not. White reversed out of black can be visually strong, but only if the right face is used. For example, a fine serif face below 12pt for large areas of text is not a good idea because the words will not be clear. Also, the quality of platemaking, and particularly the inking of the press rollers, must be perfect since there is a strong tendency for the serifs to fill in. If the typeface contains fine hairline strokes, these too can be lost.

Fenice Light

Generally speaking, black on white type is extremely legible; conversely white type reversed out of black is not. White reversed out of black can be visually strong, but only if the right face is used. For example, a fine serif face below 12pt for large areas of text is not a good idea because the words will not be clear. Also, the quality of platemaking, and particularly the inking of the press rollers, must be perfect since there is a strong tendency for the serifs to fill in. If the typeface contains fine hairline strokes, these too can be lost.

Fenice Light

Generally speaking, black on white type is extremely legible; conversely white type reversed out of black is not. White reversed out of black can be visually strong, but only if the right face is used. For example, a fine serif face below 12pt for large areas of text is not a good idea because the words will not be clear. Also, the quality of platemaking, and particularly the inking of the press rollers, must be perfect since there is a strong tendency for the serifs to fill in. If the typeface contains fine hairline strokes, these too can be lost.

Souvenir

Generally speaking, black on white type is extremely legible; conversely white type reversed out of black is not. White reversed out of black can be visually strong, but only if the right face is used. For example, a fine serif face below 12pt for large areas of text is not a good idea because the words will not be clear. Also, the quality of platemaking, and particularly the inking of the press rollers, must be perfect since there is a strong tendency for the serifs to fill in.

Bookman

Generally speaking, black on white type is extremely legible; conversely white type reversed out of black is not. White reversed out of black can be visually strong, but only if the right face is used. For example, a fine serif face below 12pt for large areas of text is not a good idea because the words will not be clear. Also, the quality of platemaking, and particularly the inking of the press rollers, must be perfect since there is a strong tendency for the serifs to fill in.

Congress

Generally speaking, black on white type is extremely legible; conversely white type reversed out of black is not. White reversed out of black can be visually strong, but only if the right face is used. For example, a fine serif face below 12pt for large areas of text is not a good idea because the words will not be clear. Also, the quality of platemaking, and particularly the inking of the press rollers, must be perfect since there is a strong tendency for the serifs to fill in.

Souvenir

Generally speaking, black on white type is extremely legible; conversely white type reversed out of black is not. White reversed out of black can be visually strong, but only if the right face is used. For example, a fine serif face below 12pt for large areas of text is not a good idea because the words will not be clear. Also, the quality of platemaking, and particularly the inking of the press rollers, must be perfect since there is a strong tendency for the serifs to fill in.

Bookman

Generally speaking, black on white type is extremely legible; conversely white type reversed out of black is not. White reversed out of black can be visually strong, but only if the right face is used. For example, a fine serif face below 12pt for large areas of text is not a good idea because the words will not be clear. Also, the quality of platemaking, and particularly the inking of the press rollers, must be perfect since there is a strong tendency for the serifs to fill in.

Congress

Generally speaking, black on white type is extremely legible; conversely white type reversed out of black is not. White reversed out of black can be visually strong, but only if the right face is used. For example, a fine serif face below 12pt for large areas of text is not a good idea because the words will not be clear. Also, the quality of platemaking, and particularly the inking of the press rollers, must be perfect since there is a strong tendency for the serifs to fill in.

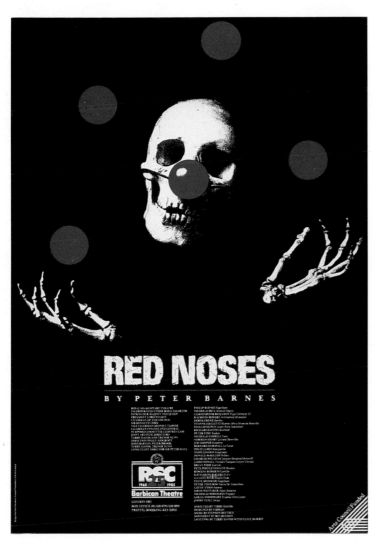

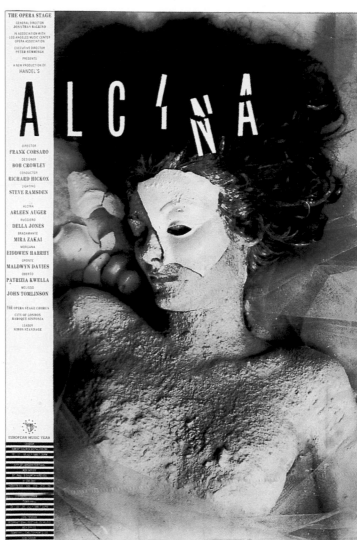

■ **Below** The headline of this striking two-color poster by Richard Mellor uses type well. The disintegration of the characters doesn't affect legibility at all, in fact it draws the eye toward it, as the designer intended. However, I would question the use of the reversed-out type in parallel blocks at the bottom. Reading type within vertical stripes is difficult enough without the reversal – but perhaps the copy isn't all that important.

■ **Above** A very powerful poster designed by the company Lloyd Northover for the Royal Shakespeare Company, using just two colors. With a concept such as this there is no way in which type could have been used in any colors other than black and white. There does seem to be rather too much to read easily, but when seen as a full-size poster this is not a serious problem.

Body copy set in the three primary colors creates similar problems to white reversed out of black, whether they are on white or reversed out of black. The bright magenta and secondary red, green and violet colors are just as tiring on the eyes, while yellow on white is far too weak in tone for any degree of reasonable legibility. To a lesser degree the same is true of cyan, although because of its recessive nature it does not strain the eyes as much. The softer dark browns and grays can work well but should really only be used in promotional material where a fifth color can be used specifically for the copy. This insures a far cleaner, crisper image than could otherwise be achieved in general magazine production, where any fifth color has to obtained by the four-color half-tone process. The screening of fine type (14pt and below) is not good design; the edges lack clarity and, again, if the registration is fractionally out, legibility suffers further.

Ossidet ignis multa, dolorem oculis quae gignunt insinuando. Lurida praeterea fiunt quaecumque tuentur arquati, quia luroris de corpore eorum semina multa fluunt simulacris.

Fugitant uitantque tueri; sol etiam caecat, contra si tendere pergas propterea quia uis magnast ipsius, et alte aera per purum saepe grauiter simulacra feruntur, et feriunt oculos turbantia composituras. Praeterea splendor quicumque est acer adurit oculos, ideo quod semina possidet ignis multa, dolorem oculis quae gignunt insinuando.

Aquati, quia luroris de corpore eorum semina multa fluunt simulacris. Culi fugitant uitantque tueri; sol etiam caecat, contra si tendere pergas propterea quia uis magnast ipsius, et alte aera per purum grauiter simulacra feruntur, et feriunt oculos turbantia composituras. Praeterea splendor quicumque est acer adurit saepe oculos, ideo quod semina.

Ossidet ignis multa, dolorem oculis quae gignunt contra insinuando. Lurida praeterea fiunt quaecumque tuentur arquati, luroris de corpore eorum semina multa fluunt simulacris.

■ **Left** The three examples reversed out of black are process colors – magenta, cyan and yellow.

■ Posters seem to lend themselves to reversing out. I like the way the Alvin Ailey design by Steff Geissbuhler **below** has created space with its openly spaced Bodoni. The example right shows how design can change by alternating colors. **Below right**, a multi-colored typeface designed by Pentagram UK breaks the rules of logic yet still works.

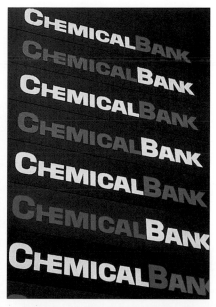

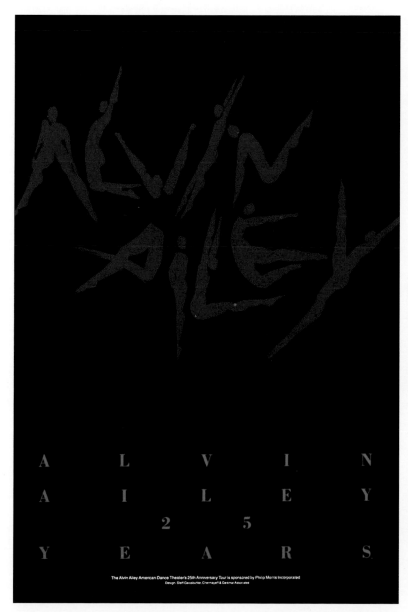

The Alvin Ailey American Dance Theater's 25th Anniversary Tour is sponsored by Philip Morris Incorporated
Design: Steff Geissbuhler, Chermayeff & Geismar Associates

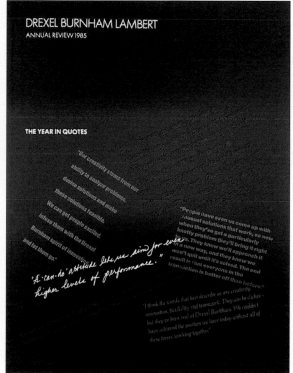

DREXEL BURNHAM LAMBERT
ANNUAL REVIEW 1985

THE YEAR IN QUOTES

Culi fugitant titantque tueri; sol etiam caecat, contra si tendere pergas propterea quia uis magnast ipsius, et alte aera per purum grauiter simulacra feruntur, et feriunt oculos turbantia composituras. Praeterea splendor qtiicumque est acer adurit saepe oculos, ideo quod semina possidet ignis multa, dolorem oculis quae gignunt insinuando. Lurida praeterea fiunt quaecumque tuentur.

Aspuit, quia luroris de corpore eorum semina multa.

Rules are made to be broken, and limited use of colored type can work, provided that the typeface is sufficiently strong for good readability and that the quantity of body copy is restricted before eye strain occurs. Obviously such thresholds can be assessed by the designer only in the context of the work in question.

Et alte aera per purum grauiter simulacra feruntur, et feriunt oculos turbantia composituras. Praeterea splendor quicumque est acer adurit saepe oculos, ideo quod semina possidet ignis multa, dolorem oculis quae gignunt insinuando.

Urida praeterea fiunt quaecumque tuentur arquati, quia luroris de corpore eorum semina multa fluunt simulacris. Spolendor quicumque est acer adurit saepe oculos, ideo quod.

■ **Left** Further examples of colored type, this time against a white background, demonstrate the legibility of colors.

Quia uis magnast ipsius, et alte aera per purum grauiter simulacra feruntur, et feriunt oculos turbantia composituras. Praeterea splendor quicumque est acer adurit saepe oculos, ideo quod semina.

Ossidet ignis multa, dolorem oculis quae gignunt insinuando. Lurida praeterea fiunt quaecumque tuentur arquati, quia luroris de corpore eorum semina multa fluunt simulacris.

■ **Left** This design really speaks for itself. Beautiful, evocative color with limited copy, creates an image that is easy to read, and restful on the eyes.

Et alte aera per purum grauiter simulacra feruntur, et feriunt oculos turbantia composituras. Praeterea splendor quicumque est acer adurit saepe oculos, ideo quod semina possidet ignis multa, dolorem oculis quae gignunt quia insinuando.

Urida praeterea fiunt quaecumque tuentur arquati, luroris de corpore eorum semina multa fluunt simulacris. Spolendor quicumque est acer adurit saepe oculos, ideo quod.

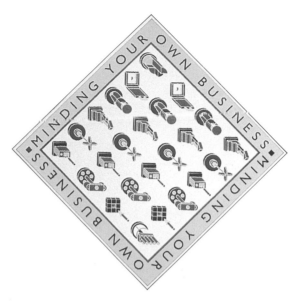

■ **Far left** A page from a small booklet promoting an Albuquerque printer. The style throughout follows the format of pure color with limited text, the purity being achieved by printing each color separately. It is an expensive method but excellent printing does cost a lot. **Left** This colored type has been tastefully handled by Grundy & Northedge. Without the subtlety of the gray tint background the lettering could have looked raw and crude.

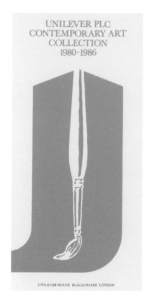

UNILEVER PLC
CONTEMPORARY ART
COLLECTION
1980-1986

UNILEVER HOUSE BLACKFRIARS LONDON

■ Two contrasting examples of colored type. **Above** This piece contains limited type and restful color which is easy on the eye. **Right** A vibrant and fiery example, but I wonder if anyone has managed to read any of the text?

There are other instances where legibility suffers that don't refer merely to reversed-out type. The most common form of type misuse is the combination of text over illustrative material. Black type over a plain dark color can read quite well, but black text over a heavily textured background, even if it's a light color, can become virtually in-decipherable. This is a very common fault, when type, particularly body copy, is combined with full-color photography, and it explains why so many art directors play safe with their advertising layouts by using the standard format of squared-up half-tones with black text on white below the illustrative matter.

■ **Right** One of the most effective ways of printing type over a textured background is to use textured paper. This delightful ticket printed in just two flat colors is a fine example of how well this can work.

BALLET

WEST

OF·NEW·MEXICO

Ballet West of New Mexico Inc., Gala
Friday Evening November 15, 1985
6:30 Cocktails   7:30 Dinner
$50 per person
Albuquerque Convention Center
Black Tie Optional

Culi fugitant uitantque tueri; sol etiam caecat, contra si tendere pergas propterea quia uis magnast ipsius, et alte aera per purum grauiter simulacra feruntur, et feriunt oculos turbantia composituras. Praeterea splendor quicumque est acer adurit saepe oculos, ideo quod semina

Black text on a light-colored texture

Possidet ignis multa, dolorem oculis quae gignunt insinuando. Lurida praeterea fiunt quaecumque tuentur. Aquati, quia luroris de corpore eorum semina multa fluunt simulacris. Culi fugitant uitantque tueri; sol etiam caecat, contra si tendere pergas propterea quia uis

Black text on a dark, flat color

Magnast ipsius, et alte aera per purum grauiter simulacra feruntur, et feriunt oculos turbantia composituras. Praeterea splendor quicumque est acer adurit saepe oculos, ideo quod semina. Ossidet ignis multa, dolorem oculis quae gignunt insinuando.

Black text on a dark texture

This is Mohawk Artemis Cover, 80 lb. Blue.

Labyrinth-Logo Typography © 1984 by Seymour Robins

■ **Left** This endpaper design is for a booklet for the Mohawk Paper Mills' graphic essay on "Mazes and Labyrinths." Seymour Robins designed the typeface specially for the project. His intention was to create a display face which contained good classic qualities yet was modern and distinctive in its usage. He has now developed a complete alphabet under the name of "Labyrinth-Logo." Since the function of this design is purely decorative, it is quite acceptable to allow the typography itself to "become" the texture.

■ **Bottom left** The masthead for the magazine *Skald* from Pentagram UK. The copy line below the main title is difficult to read over the texture, but such information normally contains minor text only and is not critical. **Below** In these two examples comprehension really does matter. My reaction to the first, which is reproduced same size, is: "When will they learn? Why make reading difficult for people?" It's just poor design. The second example is a little better as the simpler tones of the background make reading easier, but it's far from perfect.

SKALD

PREMIER ISSUE THE PUBLICATION JOURNAL FOR VIKING LINE'S SKALD CLUB MEMBERS VOL. 1, ISSUE 1 FALL 1984

WHEN PAPER IS used as a support for watercolour, or acrylic paints heavily diluted with water, it is necessary to stretch it. Basically fibres of the paper are dampened and they expand. Held in this state as the water evaporates, the resulting strain ensures that even if the paper is subjected to a heavy application of watery paint, as in a wash, the paper remains flat and does not buckle or bubble. For some people the process is stunningly easy to understand and execute. For others it is a hit and miss activity with unpredictable

the finished article will lo will have been minimal ar buckle at the merest hint o

Water can be applied w quickly moving over one s other, creating a surface wl but does not have a pool of sitting on it. The paper car tap, but care needs to be papers. The use of a tray fi often recommended, but av paper for too long. In this

THERE ARE AN enormous number of papers and boards to choose from. Not all of these are intended for artistic use, but separating out those that are is not a simple matter. This is because the use of paper by artists, illustrators and designers is not confined to drawing and painting. Even if it were, there are different types of drawing and painting using different media, which require properties

have given us its name from papyrus, the reed they used to make scrolls. Several *Books of the Dead*, a sort of Michelin guide to the afterlife, can be seen on it at the British Museum. In very general terms it resembles paper, but there is no direct connection and it was the Chinese who actually invented it. Exactly when is a moot point. 200 to 300 years BC seems probable and some examples that can be dated to that

on
ma
Or
dif
pa
the
ing
fro

The question that now needs to be posed is: *"Do art directors have to play safe to create imaginative, lively layouts?"* The answer is obviously *"No!"* But how can the designer move away from the security of the standard style and avoid the pitfalls of badly executed white out of black type, or type over complex textured backgrounds?

Of course, the actual product to be promoted does have a bearing upon the approach to the design problem. For example, automobile advertising tends to lend itself to the squared-up halftone approach where excellence of photography is a prerequisite. There are, however, countless areas of the visual communications industry where a more imaginative approach can and should be employed.

First of all, let us study the headline *"Be adventurous...Take chances"* — a suitable, short phrase for the purpose of these examples and a phrase that could be etched above the drawing boards of all creative designers (see below left). Conventionally the headline would be placed in one or two lines with close letter spacing in a strong serif face. And the color? Black of course! (Notice the kerning, in particular the "a" set under the arm of the "T.")

Although the phrase is short there is no reason why type mixing can't be employed. Variation can

"Be adventurous ...
Take chances"

"BE ADVENTUROUS...
TAKE CHANCES"

"be adventurous...
take chances"

Tuli fugitant uitantque tueri; sol etiam caecat, contra si tendere pergas propterea quia uis magnast ipsius, et alte aera per purum grauiter simulacra feruntur, et feriunt oculos turbantia composituras. Praeterea splendor quicumque est acer adurit saepe oculos, ideo quod semina possidet ignis multa, dolorem oculis quae gignunt insinuando. Lurida praeterea fiunt quaecumque

Italic with vertical alignment

Tuli fugitant uitantque tueri; sol etiam caecat, contra si tendere pergas propterea quia uis magnast ipsius, et alte aera per purum grauiter simulacra feruntur, et feriunt oculos turbantia composituras. Praeterea splendor quicumque est acer adurit saepe oculos, ideo quod semina possidet ignis multa, dolorem oculis quae gignunt insinuando. Lurida praeterea

Large initial character

WOMEN IN TRANSITION

EVERY GOODBYE AIN'T GONE
By L. Teresa Church and Ann Marie Lopes
Directed by Bistra Lankova

A Black woman, torn between an
obligation to her aging mother and her
desire for an independent life, struggles
with the changing nature of the family
and women's roles in the Afro-American
community.

February 17-26

Folkthought:
Audience Discussion · February 26, 4 pm

DANCE MAMA, DANCE
by Barbara Bejoian
Directed by Amy Lloyd

A young woman, searching for the
meaning of her Armenian heritage,
must confront her family and ethnic
history in order to realize her own life as
an Armenian-American.

April 6-15

Folkthought:
Audience Discussion · April 15, 4pm

PERFORMANCES
Friday - Sunday, 8 pm
Sunday matinee, 4 pm

Churchill House
155 Angell Street
Providence

All performances are free

Call 863-3558 for group reservations
and more information.

easily be introduced with extreme contrast of
weight. By moving away from the close spacing
and introducing a sans serif face, you can achieve a
totally different feel.

But why not introduce color as well — not
throughout, but a contrast of color together with
black and white? Roman mixed with italic will also
introduce another new variation. As you can see
from the examples, the extent of variation need be
restricted only by the designer's own limitations of
creativity.

The body copy can also be given a fresher
appearance when it moves away from orthodox
styles of setting. Black type on colored tints, italic
body copy with vertical alignment and various
forms of large first character initials all create an
unusual effect.

ENGLISH ANY TIME

JOHN DOUGILL

■ **Above** An excellent poster in
which the designer, Allen Wong of
the Brown Design group, has
cleverly integrated Caslon No 471
with Avant Garde Bold for the
main title. In spite of the 50
percent difference in size between
the two segments of each
character, legibility does not suffer.
It is another example of the
tremendous flexibility that type
allows the creative imagination.
Below the title Frutiger light and
bold is set on a 50 degree indent.

■ **Left** This striking book jacket,
designed by Crucial Books, is a
good example of the use of
vertical italic.

The style of headline does of course have to be sympathetic toward the product, but that is no reason for reduced creativity. Not only is the product important but the socio-economic groupings of the projected market and the age of the potential consumer have also to be taken into account. Promotion for the teenage market can, as you would expect, be more aggressive. Blocks of different colors behind type, a complete mix of fonts for every character, the introduction of script capitals together with sans serif characters, italic fonts with the stem aligned vertically allowing the type to run uphill — all are possibilities and can be successfully mixed when appealing to the younger generation. These same techniques can be applied to an older, more mature market, but a greater degree of restraint and sophistication does have to be employed. As the product becomes more expensive so does the style of promotion. People who can afford quality expect that same degree of quality and sophistication from their advertising and promotional material.

■ **Below** The cover and spread from I-D magazine are clearly aimed at a teenage/young twenties readership. The use of several strong colors alongside hard-hitting headlines in a sans serif face on the cover, **left**, appeals to this market and stands out from other magazines for this age group. The contents page, **right**, set in a computer face in white reversed out of the colored background, is striking but not very easy to read.

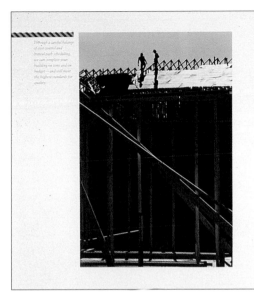

efforts of the developer, architect, and construction contractor. Through a careful balance of cost control and critical-path scheduling, we can complete your building on time and on budget — and still meet the highest standards for quality.

Our involvement in a project often begins when it is no more than an idea. At that stage, we can provide initial estimates for your budgeting purposes.

As the design is developed, we stay involved, helping to ensure that the design meets not only your construction budget, but also your budget for long-term maintenance. With our knowledge of construction and materials costs, you can make informed decisions about design options as well as marketable features and amenities.

■ The spread **left** by Blake Miller uses Serifa 45 with hung caps, giving the appearance of wooden type. In its printed size the white type works well, The Vaughn/ Wedeen design **below left** for Richard Yates Architects Inc., uses color in a much more subdued and subtle manner. Even more restrained is their brochure for the Western Bank Plaza **below**. Each page features large raised initials with very open line spacing on a gray/lilac paper opposite high-quality photography with a similar lilac tint on white. They are very tasteful designs.

THE MASTER BUILDER

Today's architect must constantly strive to keep up to date with the rapidly advancing technology in the building industry. New and better methods are always being perfected, so it is imperative to remain abreast of each and every development. Yet, in order to be truly successful, architects must not only keep pace with the present, but also understand and implement the principles of the past. At Richard Yates Architects, Inc., mastering new techniques is important, but we place an equal amount of importance on the fundamental principles that have developed throughout the history of architecture. The necessary melding of past and present is a challenge that is best understood by reflecting upon the architect of earlier times—the Master Builder.

The architecture of the Renaissance period best describes the seemingly lost art of the Master Builder. At that time, if a cathedral was able to impress the public with the vast amounts of space its vaulted ceiling enclosed, it was considered a success. Aesthetic impact was a vital part of a building's function and purpose.

Famous Renaissance buildings such as St. Peter's Cathedral were designed by architects who were primarily painters and sculptors. They were not concerned with complicated books of government building codes, or the need for electrical wiring, heat ducts and plumbing. However, a Renaissance architect was also expected to design such dissimilar projects as roads, decorations for festivals, and aqueducts and bridges. His primary role was that of an artist and an engineer. In spite of so many diverse responsibilities, the architect of the past had less concern for many of the functions that complicate the present. After all, a single building wasn't required to fulfill multiple purposes, and roads did not need to handle 18-wheelers and rush-hour traffic.

The architect of the Renaissance was more single-minded in purpose, yet less constrained by time. This enabled him to pursue a wider scope of projects while retaining full control over all aspects from inception to completion.

ARCHITECTURAL ORIGINS

"Architecture is the art which so disposes and adorns the edifices raised by man that the sight of them contributes to his mental health, power, and pleasure."

—John Ruskin

Western Bank Plaza is situated at the very pulse of downtown Albuquerque, so convenience and visibility are assured. Its close proximity to government buildings, courts and major financial headquarters positions it at the very heart of the city's central business district. Some of the city's finest restaurants, hotels, cultural centers and shopping arenas are within walking distance. Western Bank Plaza itself contains a full-service bank, sundry store and coffee shop.

Its location also provides easy access to major freeways and thoroughfares, so getting to and from work is made simple. Western Bank Plaza has five levels of covered parking with one of the highest percentages of spaces per occupant available.

The newly renovated interior of Western Bank Plaza is a study in warm, quiet elegance. The overall color scheme brings the soft hues of the desert southwest to the building's contemporary interior design. Floor coverings, wall arrangements, foliage, furniture and upholstery are all skillfully designed and arranged to achieve sophisticated warmth and tasteful charm. From the entrance level to the corridors, each detail is conspicuously created to enhance our tenants' image—so their clients receive a lasting first impression.

The Invisible Message

This section might seem a slight digression from the main subject of typography, but it is an area rarely covered in design literature, although all designers should have an appreciation and understanding of it. It is the area of "color blindness," or "color deficiency" as it should more accurately be called. Not everyone has normal color recognition — in fact, the problem affects a very large percentage of the population. The overwhelming majority of people who have some degree of color deficiency is male. The percentage of men with color blindness is somewhere between one in ten and one in twelve, whereas the percentage is as low as one in 250 with women.

Before moving onto the actual manifestations of the forms of color deficiency some general background information might be of interest to you. I hope that what I'm about to say doesn't sound too much like a section out of a medical journal, but I think it could be both beneficial and of general interest.

Color vision is defined as the ability to perceive hue, color brightness, and color saturation corresponding to the normal visible wavelengths between the infra-red and ultra-violet bands of the light spectrum. Normal vision can distinguish around 160 basic shades.

The most common colors that people have problems differentiating are red and green. Only a very small percentage of people have difficulty with yellow and blue. Total color blindness is almost completely unknown. Figures as low as one in 100,000,000 are quoted for those who see life in monochromatic tones only.

It appears that more of the people who suffer from a red-green deficiency live in the developed world, as opposed to peoples such as the Australian aborigines and native Indians of the South and North Americas. It is interesting to note that the red-green deficiency is higher in Europe, becoming more manifest in groups where there is a high degree of inter-breeding such as with the Merronites, Mormons and similar groups. This is perhaps not so surprising when you know that color deficiency is an hereditary congenital disorder, transmitted through the X-chromosome. This particular chromosome is recessive in the female, which explains why color deficiency is low in women. Unfortunately for people born with color deficiency there is no cure, as it is caused by a defect in the light-sensitive cells of the retina.

As you would expect, certain careers demand a perfect sense of color recognition. Pilots, naval

■ **Right** These two photographs of a bowl of fruit, which are actually identical, show **left** how color is perceived by people with normal vision, and **right**, how it is seen by those with a red color deficiency.

officers and train drivers all have to pass the appropriate tests; electricians also need to be able to distinguish between the different color codes of wiring. Obviously in the field of design it is also important, but not necessarily vital. Interior and fashion designers need a perfect color sense, but there is no reason why copywriters and, to a lesser extent, typographers should not be able to have successful careers in the communications industry with some degree of color deficiency. It is an interesting theory, but women do seem to be extremely successful in certain areas of the design world where a greater degree of color sensitivity is required. One must assume that there is a strong link between this and the extremely low numbers of women who suffer from color deficiency.

But how does all this affect the designer? I'm not suggesting that everything you design should be directed away from certain color combinations, but an understanding of the common problems of color deficiency, and its manifestations, could mean a subtle change of color here and there to your designs, which would make them just that little bit easier to be understood by everyone. After all, who wants to lose 10 percent of their readers even before they start?

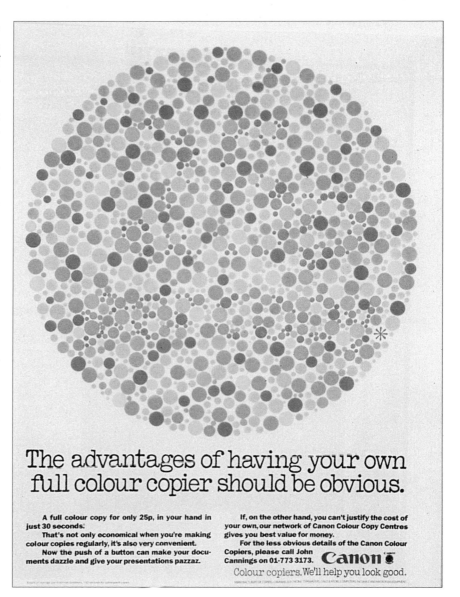

The advantages of having your own full colour copier should be obvious.

A full colour copy for only 25p, in your hand in just 30 seconds.
That's not only economical when you're making colour copies regularly, it's also very convenient.
Now the push of a button can make your documents dazzle and give your presentations pazzaz.

If, on the other hand, you can't justify the cost of your own, our network of Canon Colour Copy Centres gives you best value for money.
For the less obvious details of the Canon Colour Copiers, please call John Cannings on 01-773 3173. **Canon**

Colour copiers. We'll help you look good.

■ **Above** An advertisement to promote Cannon color copiers. It is an interesting idea, but what about those readers who suffer from a green color deficiency? It must surely defeat the object of the exercise if you're going to produce an ad that some people won't be able to understand!

■ **Right** These examples illustrate exactly what I mean. The four stamp designs, conceived by Tayburn and illustrated by Magnus Lohkamp, were issued by the British Post Office to portray medieval life. If you look at the 17p stamp **below right** it contains areas of similar values of red and green set against an ocher background. People with a green or red deficiency would find it extremely difficult to distinguish between the trees on the slopes and the birds in the tree. With due respect to the designer of an otherwise delightful design, a small modification to the values of these colors could have helped their appreciation by another 10 percent of the population. The illustration **below** shows how the stamp would look to someone with a green deficiency.

TRANSLATING INTO BLACK AND WHITE

As if it is not enough to think about the readability of type in color, designers also have to be aware of how legible their designs will be when converted into black and white. Although a very high percentage of television sets in the western world are now in full color, there is still an exceptionally large number of monochromatic sets in regular use. In addition leaflets, books and magazines often contain black and white reproductions of work originally designed in color, and most advertising at some stage is reproduced in black and white. If the color values are not well-balanced, the message will be illegible in black and white.

■ **Above and left** This color design by Grundy & Northedge for the Contemporary Art Society has used a strong blue – normally recessive – with a weak orange – normally dominant. When copied monochromatically the blue recedes and the red content in the orange starts to advance. This then produces a reasonably balanced design in its new monochromatic form.

COLOR
Mood and message

Part Two: **Introduction**

Now for color. The most interesting aspect of the subject, but one that can easily lead you to make the wrong choice, is that it can be all things to all people. Green, for example, can be perceived as violent and exciting, a color that signals an alert (as in traffic lights), and one that can be associated with envy, disease and decay. On the other hand it can signify calm and peace, having associations with nature and the countryside and a healthy way of living. This wealth of symbolic associations is shared by all the other colors in the spectrum.

With just this one example it's easy to see how color added to type increases the message of the type and is therefore an essential part of the design. But it will work only if the designer understands the properties of the color and the effect he or she is trying to create.

The following chapters take you through the range of aspects that have to be considered when choosing a color: its symbolic associations; its

Have a break.

volume and vibrancy — does it shout? Is it bright? Or is it pale and soft? Its temperature — is it warm, or cool? Its market appeal — is it stylish or cheap? Is its image one of tradition, security and dependability, or is it modern, dynamic and innovative? And lastly, its decorative value. In each chapter I have selected examples that compare the different uses of color and the variety of effects that are achieved, from travel brochures and promotions to the packaging of food products, pharmaceutical and natural health products, advertisements for the arts and other forms of entertainment, engineering, cosmetics and sports.

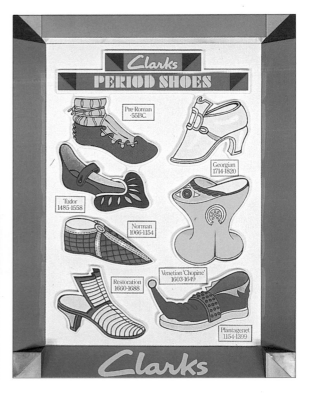

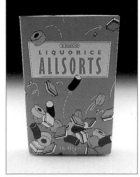

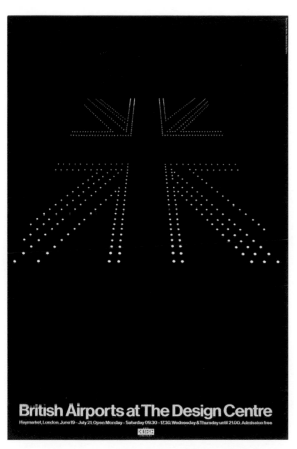

■ These images illustrate the wide scope of color in typographic design, from billboards to packaging, calendars to posters.

Seeing red!

Many colors have messages that are internationally recognized and symbolize various actions, warnings, or products the world over. The most obvious example is the code for traffic signals: red for stop, green for go. Although it is very easy to fall into the trap of generalizations, colors do have certain properties that remain the same through the pendulum swings of fashion that affect other aspects of color, such as acceptability and popularity. It is these properties that convey the message of each color.

By "properties" I mean aspects such as volume, excitement value, temperature, and symbolic value. Let's start with volume. There are quiet colors, such as light blue, light pink, and soft gray, and there are loud colors, such as bright reds and bright greens. Their *"volume"* comes from their dominance (how much they seem to jump out at you), or from their recessiveness (how much they sink into the background). Dominant, or loud, colors are aggressive, whereas recessive, or paler, colors are passive.

You might use quiet colors for a product such as a fabric softener, with its connotations of soft blankets and woolens, but it is unlikely that you would use loud colors for such a product. You might use loud colors for a food product, such as salt, which will appear on the supermarket shelves among containers full of the same product, and choose bright colors such as red and bright blue on white, simply so that your product will stand out from all the rest.

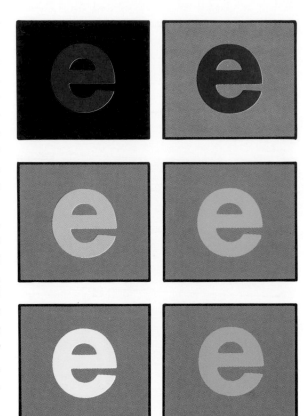

This set of six letters illustrates how color dominance can vary depending on the color it is set against. The red on the gray background, is very much more strident than the pink, blue, yellow and green on the same background. These techniques of color contrast and blending are used extensively in packaging design, as will be illustrated throughout this chapter.

Of course there are other considerations to be taken into account when choosing a color, and they all combine to create the final product, but each must be assessed on its own before the whole is put together. So, on to the next — *excitement value*. "Excitement" can refer to warning, danger, risk, and fear. The colors used most commonly to signify excitement are red and orange, used extensively in the areas of poisons and lethal chemicals, explosives and road hazards; but, particularly in the case of red, they also represent blood, horror and revolution. Conversely, for products with no excitement value, a designer may want to put across the opposite image and use safe colors. These are usually blues, browns, dark greens or grays.

■ **Left** Black and red are traditional warning colors, found in nature and in our cultural symbolism. Red is an easy color to see, particularly from a distance, and is therefore commonly used to signify potentially hazardous areas on the road or the sidewalk.

■ **Below** This sign outside the Rockefeller Center, New York, is a pleasing design which commands attention mainly by its good taste. The introduction of a warm brown blends well with the surrounding environment.

■ **Left** These warning signs are typical of the ways in which color is used in this context. Red has always been the international code for road hazards, but warning codes have now been extended to include a black and yellow scheme for poisons, toxic fumes and radiation risks. Orange is a loud color and allows the message to be read more clearly.

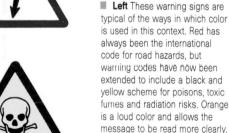

Color temperature

Colors also have *temperatures*: yellow, orange, red, purple and pink tend to be warm, whereas blue and green are cold. However, the shades of each color of the spectrum can have a temperature that is the opposite to that of its pure color — a pale yellow, a pale pink or lilac can be cool, whereas a yellow-green can be warm. The temperature of colors is significant in designs where you might want to indicate heat, such as in travel brochures which advertise vacations in the sun, or coolness, such as in an advertisement for a refreshing drink.

■ **Below** This typographic design from Tim Girvin Design is an interesting example of color and temperature change within a single image. It moves from the heat of the bright red through to what would normally be termed cold white, but here the title itself sets up an association with white heat, so that the color is "warmed" by the mind.

■ **Above** This example, also from Tim Girvin Design, is really self-explanatory in both color and typographic use.

■ **Left** By contrast, this example from Minale, Tattersfield has used warm colors in a quite different way – here they suggest the freshness of fruit.

The *symbolic properties* of colors are the most readily recognizable — we are all aware that light green conveys an image of tranquillity and calm, blue signifies water and hygiene, orange and yellow suggest the sun, purple has overtones of pomp and ceremony, and browns are harvest colors. Color can have symbolic value in every area from natural health to medicine, politics to sport. I have chosen the following examples from several of these areas to demonstrate color association with product, and also to point out the anomalies.

Above The chocolate box from David Davies places green alongside white and a cool gray, as opposed to a warm gray, to create the right cool temperature for a mint-flavored product.

Feminine colors

Colors can be used to suggest gentleness and caring, and can be associated with feminity and motherhood. Such associations occur most frequently in the area of packaging, particularly in the promotion of items for the home and for young children. The tendency is to choose pastel shades for such promotions, and designers rely heavily on light pastel pinks, blues and yellows, often with a hint of gray within their basic palette.

■ **Above and right** These two examples of packaging by Coley Porter Bell are for similar products but their color schemes create totally different moods. The softer design for the "Moods" air fresheners has color associations with spring mornings/summer days/autumn evenings, whereas the stronger colors on the stick-ups are far less subtle in their message.

■ **Above and right** Here is another contrast in approach. Both examples use pastel colors, but one product is to be sold through a chain of upmarket outlets, whereas the other is aimed at high-volume supermarket sales. The Next range of body products, **above**, designed by David Davies, uses very subtle color changes and has very elegant appeal, whereas the colors of the Asda fabric conditioner packs from Lloyd Northover, **right**, are far brighter, though still using basic pinks and blues to stress softness. They are thus more suitable to the high-volume competition on the supermarket shelf.

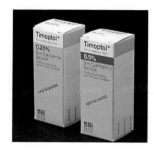

Above Generally speaking a much heavier design approach is required for most pharmaceutical packaging than for softer, more soothing products. But the two packs by Minale. Tattersfield for Timoptol, in pale gray/blue and gray/pink manage to stress the gentle action of the product while retaining a clean and clinical look.

ALZA ANNUAL REPORT 1984

ALZA's rate controlled therapeutic systems are designed to improve treatment while reducing side effects—thus leading to happier as well as healthier lives for many patients.

Left The cover design for this drug company report was produced by Pentagram UK. The whole of this publication stresses the concept of care, and this is reflected in the colors used, as well as in the choice of illustrated material and the restrained typography. This restraint is typified by the white out of pale blue.

Below The logo for the Cooperative Health Care Plan Inc. shows an alternative approach to suggesting cleanliness and efficiency – pale colors on a gray ground.

THE NEW GUIDE TO WOMEN'S HEALTH

— Norma Williams MD and Hetty Einzig —

A positive new approach to health care for women • How to monitor your own health • The fertile years • Sexuality and partnerships • What it means to be female • The working woman • Enjoying the later years • Advice on pregnancy • How to get the best from your doctor • Diet and fitness • Helpful diagrams and photographs

Left Although bright colors could have worked for this book jacket because health is a lively subject, it was decided to use softer colors, which are associated with the gentle treatment of pregnant women.

COOPERATIVE HEALTH CARE

Fresh colors

Color is also used to suggest freshness, with bright blues, greens and yellows being the colors most often chosen where vitality and sparkle are associated with the product. Obviously, where there is an association with fresh water and coolness, blue has a prominent role, as does green for the promotion of field sports and other outdoor pursuits. Fresh fruit and vegetables, which stress freshness and goodness ask for the same kind of treatment, stressing freshness and goodness.

The use of pastel colors is also much in evidence in packaging for pharmaceutical products, but the nature of some products, such as medicines, demands that they be presented in a bright, fresh, clean manner, suggesting much the same quality of health associated with eating fresh fruit and salads.

■ **Above** These pack designs for "Slip Not" boat mats, designed by Lloyd Northover, combine the obvious color-association of nautical sports with the safety aspect of the product. Set against a blue background, the letter O takes the form of a lifebuoy with a red spot, for danger, inside it.

■ **Above** The use of a strong refreshing blue as a background color to this display of foot-spray products designed by The Partners works well because clear blue suggests cleanliness and coolness.

■ **Right** Predominantly blue and yellow, the Martini drink ads concentrate very much upon the "cool and fresh" approach, combined with the theme of swimming and sunbathing.

Below Products like these also need to be marketed with a "cool and fresh" image. These pack designs, by Minale,Tattersfield for the Boots "Shapers" products, stress their qualities by the use of the appropriate colors for each flavor.

SUTHERLAND HAWES DESIGN
NORTH MIDDLESEX
JUNIOR TOURNAMENT 1983
10TH ANNIVERSARY
FROM MONDAY 25TH – 30TH JULY

LTA APPROVED

Left This design by Fitch for the sporting goods section at the Samaritaine department store uses the obvious color choice – blue – to good effect.

Above right This poster design by Richard Mellor continues the natural theme of green as a sports color. For a tennis tournament poster it would have been quite difficult for the designer to have used any other colors.

Left This brochure for Artemide Lighting, by Richard Mellor, uses the same colors as the tennis poster above, but the designer *could* have used any combination of bright colors because there are no particular colors associated with light.

Above In Banks's & Hanson's real ale poster the earthy colors, nostalgic use of ceramic tiles and mock-Victorian letter forms are all a quite deliberate attempt to convey the feeling of traditionally brewed beer. The advertising agency was TBWA.

Right In this interesting logo for the Sanbusco Market Center, type style and colors combine to capture the feel of the Old West.

Healthy colors

Not all health foods are promoted with bright colors. Following the current trends toward healthy eating habits we are now eating more and more cereal products. This has led designers to gravitate toward the subtleties of earthy browns and ochers to promote many "traditional" products, which are much more in vogue now than they were in the past. Such colors are used not only to symbolize the natural, organic and healthy aspects of the produce but also to suggest tradition and evoke feelings of nostalgia. Other earthy colors used in this context are dark greens, deep golds and dark reds.

■ **Left** Smiths' Do-It-All chain market their own range of gardening products. These David Davies designs combine a 1980s style of typography with traditional woodcut illustrations which, combined with the earthy colors, create a definite up-market "organic" look. The use of more saturated colors **below left** gives these Fine Fare beer kit packs greater mass-market appeal than the gardening products. The design comes from Coley Porter Bell.

■ **Left** These designs were produced by Minale, Tattersfield for the Boots "Second Nature" wholefoods packs. It's not just the earthy colors that are important here; the visual imagery is equally so. The wicker basket, wheat grains, honeycomb and fresh fruit are all important elements in developing the visual idea.

■ **Above** Coley Porter Bell's flour pack designs for Jordans have a similar approach to the Boots example, again stressing the health-food angle. The customary colors (ie. red and blue) associated with flour bags for sale in a supermarket would not work for this "wholefood" market or for this design.

Vibrant colors

Just because current trends are moving very much toward the use of pastel and earthy colors doesn't mean that there is no longer a need for strong, bright ones. There will always be an occasion to suit a particular color scheme, and strong, vibrant colors will always find their place — the pure primary and secondary colors with little or no subtle variations, the reds, blues and yellows from which are made the secondary greens, oranges and purples. These are the attention-getters — the powerful communicators.

■ **Above** The cover for a piece of literature publicizing the developments in London's West India Dock Development Corporation. This attractive and well-balanced Fitch design uses a traditional motif and face but the colors are eye-catching.

■ **Above right** Trickett & Webb designed this simple but striking poster for an exhibition of 20th-century chairs at the RIBA (Royal Institute of British Architects). The use of a solid, primary yellow as a background for the chunky type creates a strong image which can be used for a variety of carriers such as swing tags and the catalog cover.

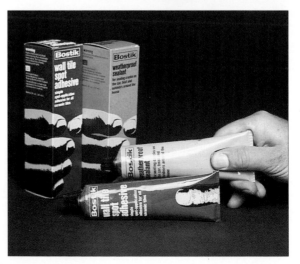

■ **Left and right** Two bright pack designs from Minale, Tattersfield. The soft drink can, **right**, has obvious color associations, but the colors for the adhesive packs, **left**, have been chosen purely for their attention-drawing qualities; they need to be noticed on the store shelves.

Right These discordant colors used on Kronen Audio stationery have been used to create an exciting visual effect in the modern idiom. However, I feel that reading a long letter on such a color might be tiring and difficult.

Below The designer may possibly have chosen blue because of its satellite and sky associations, but the contrast of white against blue makes the message shout out in an extremely effective way.

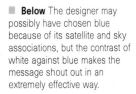

Left Logos for political parties must project a specific image and be distinctive from those of other parties. Although the flag of the British Labour Party stood out, it looked rather too revolutionary and has recently been replaced by a red rose logo. The emblem of the SDP/Liberal Alliance is a far more staid and straightforward design.

Above The style of this four-sheet poster for Persil washing powder is typical of the J. Walter Thompson approach to promoting this particular product. Good, strong vibrant colors are all contrasted against the brightness of white.

Exciting colors

So far the color schemes illustrated have been fairly controlled, and have fallen into various categories, such as pastel, earthy, vibrant, and so on. But what of multicolor projects? A fresh and courageous approach to color application can open new doors, and color can be used in a fun way to evoke moods of elation, frivolity or excitement. The implementation of such color schemes, however, can be extremely difficult, and mishandling can prove disastrous. Among the many pitfalls are imbalance, loss of clarity, and color clashes, but it should be mentioned that color discord can sometimes be used deliberately to create tension and heighten the mood of excitement. The applications of such color schemes are numerous, and can often be seen on billboards and supermarket packaging where striking colors are essential in a fiercely competitive environment.

■ **Above** The brightly colored snack food packs designed by Fitch for the Marks & Spencer chain are typical of designs for products which require high-profile shelf exposure.

■ **Right** Washing powder cartons commonly feature bright colors to reinforce the vision of dazzlingly clean clothes. These packs from Lloyd Northover are among the brightest of all.

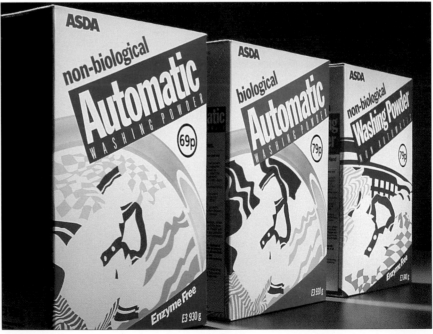

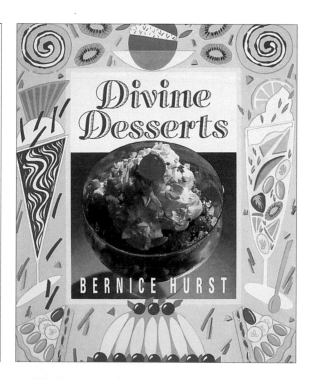

ROYAL CARIBBEAN ✠ CRUISES

■ **Left** This tantalizing book jacket, designed by Peter Bridgewater Associates, uses color well to evoke the sweetness and light of desserts. It provides a good background to the title of the book which, set in a dark brown, suggests chocolate.

■ **Above** One of the Royal Caribbean Cruise posters by the advertising agency, Travis, Dale & Partners. This example uses color primarily to create a mood of fun, warmth and relaxation, as does the handwritten catch line. Most holiday advertising is published mid-winter when bright and varied color schemes cannot fail to attract the attention of sun-hungry people.

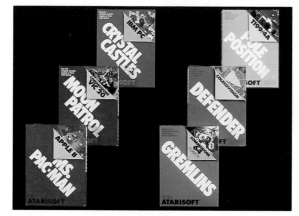

■ **Above** Each of the Atari computer game packs has a simple design featuring one dominant bright color which conveys a sense of fun and excitement.

■ **Right** The green and pink type for the passion-fruit drink Maracuja enhances the exotic, tropical nature of the drink.

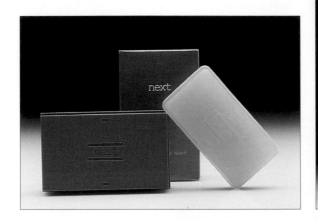

■ **Above and right** These packaging examples for Next and Giorgio Armani by David Davies make effective use of minimal color. The packaging for the soap and hair gel are aimed specifically at men, and although the Giorgio Armani packs are aimed at both sexes, they are still packed in typically "masculine" colors. A little more color is introduced into the Packman Grey food jars, but it is very muted and relies mainly on the strong black of the typography. The inclusion of the stripes tends to give a more masculine feel.

All the designs on this page are from David Davies, except the two "Pepe Grafters" swing tickets, which were designed by Worthington. Their two-color style puts them very much into the same category as the Davies examples.

Masculine colors

As we move toward the end of this chapter let us look into the more restricted uses of color and ways in which its message is put across. As often as not, economy is a reason for a reduction in color, but this is not always so, and there are instances where, although four-color reproduction has been available, the designers have deliberately opted for a more monochromatic approach. This can be seen particularly in the packaging of men's wear products, where a strong message of masculinity, or sometimes sophistication, is often required. It is also evident in the corporate image of some companies who wish to convey an image of solid ·dependability, rather than colorful frivolity.

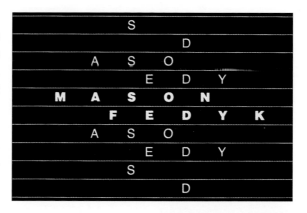

■ **Left** A single-color design for Mason Fedyk by Richard Mellor. Although it is a simple white-out-of-black design and uses a basic sans serif typeface, its appearance is both sophisticated and masculine.

■ **Right** Although typographically rather dull, the use of color here is quite unusual for a business card. There is almost a suggestion of the formal clothes and "old school tie" of the bearer.

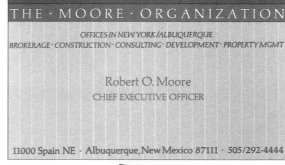

■ **Left** The Boots gift towel pack by Trickett & Webb is the only example here to use saturated color – red – but it still works in the context of the other colors – black, brown and dark blue.

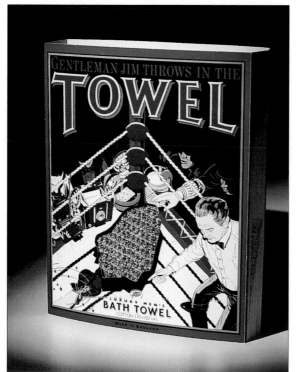

■ **Right** These packs by Minale, Tattersfield for Harrods continue the themes of formality and dark colors to create a masculine image.

■ **Right** The Suchard chocolate pack designed by Minale, Tattersfield uses gold with brown so that the browns are clean rather than earthy and give an impression of smoothness and high quality. Similarly, the jacket for the Roux Brothers' book on patisserie, **far right**, incorporates marbled paper and gold together with classic typography to enhance its perceived value.

■ **Above** The Louis Vuitton shopping bags designed by Fitch use brown in a similar manner to the Suchard pack. The discreet type treatment heightens the sophisticated effect.
Right The colors, gray, silver, gold, black, maroon, royal blue, cream, brown and dark green are synonymous with opulence and give a sophisticated upmarket effect when used with restraint in a design.

Sophisticated colors

Finally, we come to the use of color to create the impression of opulence, sophistication and high quality. Such color schemes invariably contain quantities of gold or silver, which are often mixed with other colors to create metallic blues, browns, grays and maroons. There are no rules for such schemes, as no single product has a monopoly on the suggestion of quality. A color scheme which might at first sight suggest high-quality automobiles can apply equally well to mint chocolates, bath fragrances or expensive wines, indeed any commodity where an upmarket profile is needed.

■ **Above left** The music-program cover by Cope Woollcombe & Partners creates an atmosphere of sophistication by the use of gold with black in the overall pattern and graphics from the Vienna Secession. **Above** Coley Porter Bell's butter pack is included here purely for the gold, which lifts its perceived value. Without it this would be a mundane design in fresh, spring colors. **Left** In the design of the "Country Houses of England" portfolio, by Grundy & Northedge, the marbled paper is used again, to hint at tradition and quality.

■ **Above** The Johnnie Walker Label Scoth pack (Minale, Tattersfield) uses gold and black to create an image of sophistication. In the same way marbled paper **above left**, used for Harrods' chocolate packs and designed by Minale, Tattersfield, lifts these chocolates out of the ordinary.

The color of your money

When you are designing type with color you have to bear in mind the market at which the product is aimed. You are relying on color association of a different sort — the image conveyed by the color, whether it be one of status, fun, glamor, dynamism, security or tradition. This is in turn affected by the social group the product is directed at. It is also affected by the product itself — a sophisticated color for one product may look vulgar when used in conjunction with another.

The markets you have to consider are varied and include such opposites as young or old, affluent or low-income, glamorous or earthy, national or international character, classic or modern. For

■ Right and left The transformation in the packaging of Guinness. The post-war design, **far left**, was updated in the 70s, by J. Walter thompson, **left**, to appeal to young sophisticates. They introduced a new modern typeface – Hobbs Stencil – based on stencil lettering and changed the colors so that the black and red stood out against the cream background. The label was strong then, but ten years later it seemed brash. Coley Porter Bell redesigned the new label, **below left and right**. They reintroduced the oval shape from the original label, and the caption "Brewers since 1759," but modified the Hobbs Stencil face subtly to produce a lighter, less chunky style. The cream background was replaced by a dark one and the oval now contains a manuscript yellow, giving a more traditional feel.

example, you may choose to design a poster advertising a pop concert using fluorescent pinks, oranges and greens because you know that these aggressive colors attract attention and, moreover, will appeal to the age group that will want to go to the concert. But you would not use these colors for a poster advertising a sing-along for 60-year-olds.

Every product in which graphic design is of vital importance is affected by these considerations, from the automobile industry to banking, engineering to fashion, cosmetics to food products. I've selected examples of the various images and products to demonstrate how colors do and don't work, in portraying the right image. However, I think it is a good idea if you select images from magazines or posters and analyze them yourself in terms of the characteristics I've mentioned, and try out different colors to see what differences the color changes make.

■ **Right** This traditional wine label, for Baron de Luze Claret, uses upmarket colors (gold and maroon) and classical typography. **Right center** Two 4-color labels for a downmarket German table wine use brighter, more robust colors. They make an interesting comparison with the austere but classy calligraphic label for a Californian champagne **far right**.

■ **Below** Dark colored bottles and cool label tones suggest a cold, refreshing drink. The interesting point is that the drink is non-alcoholic, but uses colors associated with alcoholic drinks to attract consumers of these drinks.

It's stating the obvious but every person in the world has to consume food and drink — without them there would be no life. But it's difficult to form a color association with a food or drink other than its natural color. However, even these basic commodities have fallen into the hands of the market strategists and every edible and drinkable substance now has an association with a particular class, age group, culture, wealth, etc. It is these values that are conveyed by typography and design.

■ **Right** The soft, laid-back colors and cookie-colored type on the these Harrod's cookie tins evoke the country goodness of homemade cookies.

■ **Right** Ice cream cone packs designed by Minale, Tattersfield. The blue, pink and yellow, and the soft browns, are appropriate to the product, as is the gold and silver aluminum, which hints at the iciness of the ice cream.

■ **Right** Designed by John Brimacombe and Company, this is a fun use of type. The white type stands out very well against the dark background, creating the appropriate ghostly effect.

JACKSONS of PICCADILLY

JACKSONS OF PICCADILLY

Above and right The development in the packaging for Jacksons of Piccadilly's range of quality teas, designed by Coley, Porter, Bell. The sample packs **top right** were a progression from the original logo, **above**. They illustrate modern packaging but don't have quite the right feel for a quality tea product – the type and the colored illustrations are too heavy, and not subtle enough. The dummy pack **far right** is a more refined design, using restrained, dark colors, but

it's lifeless and wouldn't stand out well on the shelves. The final results did pass the test though. The herbal teas **right** are colorful but with a light, delicate touch, and have the suggestion of country goodness synonymous with a herbal product. The real teas, **below right**, have a dark background which gives a feeling of quality,.but the subtly colored illustration makes them distinctive.

Left At the bottom end of the market, color is used more vividly for the bright red Typhoo pack. This is a hard sell.

Household products and toiletries

Like food and drink, color can be associated with toiletries and general household products. The function of toiletries is hygiene and cleanliness, and it therefore follows that their colors and images must portray those same values. In general, out go the blacks, grays and dirty browns and in come the pastel tones, the creams, whites, etc. But household items are so varied that you can't really define any one area of value or image, and fashions dictate to some extent which colors you use.

■ **Above** A fine example of the use of pastels in a new skin-care range designed for Almay by Fisher, Ling and Bennion. The design brief required the designer Bill Jones to produce an upmarket image to reflect the range's prime position. This sophisticated solution links products, with no range title, by image and design only. I like the clever use of the triangle, symbolizing an A, to denote the company name.

■ **Left** A good example by Lloyd Northover of how a color scheme can be rotated to produce color-coded packs. The colors are deliberately soft, reflecting the airiness of these various hair mousse products.

■ **Above** You could cover the label of this product completely and it would still say, "These contents are spring fresh." This design by Pentagram UK for Clairol is a superb use of bright, fresh colors and clean type.

Left This is an interesting choice of color scheme for a range of kitchen utensils. Trickett & Webb have not used the obvious, more common bright colors but their monochromatic approach works. It gives the impression of hygiene, cleanliness and modernity. The choice of the sans serif typeface is very important in this overall effect.

Below An example from a new series of packs to promote Action GT toys, designed by Minale, Tattersfield & Partners. The approach was one of "honesty," of not resorting to exaggerated, overdramatic and gaudy drawings, but instead to present photographs of the game or toy being played with, with obvious enjoyment.

Right The colors associated with irons need to be handled with care and control. This particular packaging is recent and is an attempt to update Morphy Richards' dull and old-fashioned image. The new look, including the re-design of the company's logo, moved the brand upmarket at the same time retaining its traditionally sympathetic and friendly image.

Right A series of microwave packs designed by Trickett & Webb. The minimal use of color gives a cool feel to the packs, but this serves to convey an image of quality, aided by the open spacing of the type.

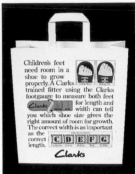

A fun approach to packaging for children's shoes by Pentagram UK for the Clarks shoe company. **Above** the use of flat, strong colors – green, red and yellow – appeals to children and catches their attention, while at the same time establishing a corporate identity for Clarks. The motif of a square divided into two triangles was derived from children's colored blocks, and is repeated on all the packaging. It was adapted for the lettering on the shoeboxes, **right**, which appears as a stenciled typeface on a colored block. The colors on the boxes work well because they serve to color-code the shoe sizes and form a colorful frieze along the walls. These colors work equally well on the Clarks shopping bag, **above right**, which includes a particularly nice touch, with good strong typography explaining the reasons for sensible foot care.

Clothing

As far as the industrial world is concerned and, increasingly, the Third World, it's not possible to sell any item of clothing in realistic production quantities without a full understanding of current fashions in color, function and age groups. Color associations for clothing cut across all sections of society — rich or poor, young or old. Many people use fashion as a means of trying to improve their self-confidence and respect, or to make a statement about themselves and it is these psychological aspects that are exploited in design.

The biggest area in fashion for variation within color values and image is age groups. From children's clothes to teenagers' garments, twenties to middle and old age, the colors and images are radically different.

■ **Above**, a fine illustration of how current graphic trends can be applied to store frontage design. Modern pastel tones are used to tone down the plain blue of the torn paper style background.
Above right Burberrys have used very upmarket, simple, classic typography and good, strong but plain color.

■ **Left** The common design feature of blue jeans is their fabric and their color, and there is little to identify one maker's blue jeans from another's. Levi's have solved this problem by concentrating on the hardwearing toughness of jeans. Their hard-hitting caption reinforces the image of their product.

■ **Above** The pastel tones of Burton's store fronts are echoed in these packs for their own-brand tights, at the same time conveying the softness of their product and an upmarket image. In contrast, the colors used for the packaging of Pex children's socks, **above left**, are bright and primary – children's colors, if you like – the colors serving as an identification of foot size.

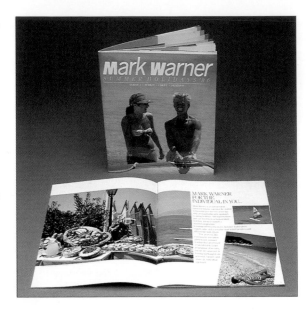

■ **Right** The selling of the dream.
Typical examples of promotional
material for annual vacations. The
prominent color scheme always
includes the use of clean blues,
with not a cloud in sight. The
prerequisite of practically any
vacation is fine weather, and this
is what the brochure designers
are promoting. The blue chosen
for winter activity is clean and
crisp – it contains an air of
freshness – whereas the blues
chosen for traditional sunbathing
holidays are warmer, and oranges
and warm yellows usually find
their way into the layout to
increase this feeling.

Travel is concerned with the promotion and selling of a dream, the dream of escape, something new, different, and perhaps exciting, away from the routine of normal day to day living. But it means different things to different people and this affects the colors that are associated with each kind of vacation that is promoted. To some, leisure means sunbathing and swimming, therefore the colors must convey a feeling of warmth and rest; to others it means winter sports, and similarly the colors must reflect the winter environment and activities; others enjoy a rest in the countryside and the colors again must convey a sense of peace and tranquillity. The graphic designer's palette must sell the particular travel activity, the individual's own particular dream.

CUNARD HAVE ALWAYS MADE A SONG AND DANCE ABOUT THEIR PASSENGERS.

■ **Left** This design understands fully where its market lies. The choice of colors and typeface, its generous spacing, the clean uncluttered layout, and the high-quality photography all evoke the golden years of sea travel and promote a similar sense of opulence now.

Art and entertainment

Art and entertainment promotion is very much to do with the creation of mood. The imagery, combined with the relevant color scheme, has to appeal to the senses, it has to provide an expectation, promise a new experience in much the same way as travel promotion does. Color use for film and drama must suggest the visual story, whether it is drama, tragedy, comedy, farce, modern, or traditional. Similarly, for music, the appropriate colors should be used — loud, vibrant, soothing, discordant, avant garde or traditional.

■ **Above and above right** Two contrasting styles of poster. Although the "Sid & Nancy" poster contains modern colors which appeal to the younger audience at which the film is aimed, overall it is restrained alongside the disturbing design of the "The Draughtman's Contract." I would have preferred the latent violence of the "Contract" poster for the Sid Vicious example – it would have been much more appropriate.

■ **Right** A poster advertising an exhibition at the Boiler House, about good and bad taste. The Roman T, made out wood, symbolizes good taste, and the furry E on the trashcan, bad taste. As an overall design it is quite stunning.

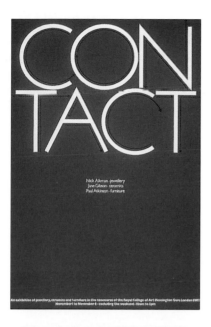

■ **Below**, the classic yellow and black caption identified with Deutsche Grammophon has become a distinctive trademark associated with classical music (it makes a good foil for the medieval romp beneath it). On the other hand, the cool gray and white and widely spaced type on the Eurythmics disk, **right**, establishes it as a modern, sophisticated production.

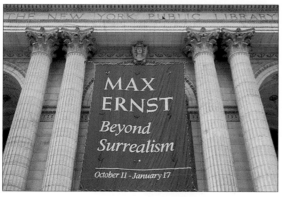

■ **Top and above** These posters for fine art exhibitions are very similar in that they both have a background of dark sophisticated color with strong typographic titles. I like the shadows on the word "Contact," created by the red arrows, which emphasize the title even further. The "Max Ernst" poster plays safer, sticking to a classic Roman and italic typeface.

■ Two designs by Vaughn Wedeen Creative, Inc. **Above right** Classical flourishes soften a strong, condensed, serif face, and muted greens and reds create a cool, elegant effect. The brochure, **right**, has used classic images with a humorous touch and with modern pastel colors.

■ **Below** Normally, magazines
are designed against unrealistic
deadlines. But for in-house
quarterlies more attention can be
given to refinement, as shown in
the well-considered run-around
type, in this spread from Skald,
the in-house magazine for the
"Royal Viking Line" pleasure
cruise company.

Publications

All that is applicable to art and entertainment in the use of colors in typography is also relevant to the world of publishing. There are thousands upon thousands of daily, weekly, monthly and quarterly publications all over the world, describing everything from computer software to botanical shrubs, from herbal remedies to the "Life & Times of Mickey Mouse." They are aimed at every conceivable section of society, and suggest every kind of mood and image. Again it's the designer's function to evoke the appropriate feel and color association for each particular product.

■ **Left** In the case of a monthly magazine such as "Elle," time considerations are more in evidence. Even so, this particular magazine, which is aimed at upmarket women, must maintain certain standards of design and creativity. This particular spread has moved away from the general style of the magazine in an attempt to create a fresher, livelier layout, and a design suitable to the particular article.

■ **Left and far left** A book cover and double-page spread which show a rather striking style for book production. The text reversed out of the black ground on the cover looks good, but generally speaking readability does suffer quite considerably. In this case the strong flat colors of the stencil typeface stand out well on the background and would be eye-catching in any bookstore. The red grid on the spread works well to delineate the columns of text and lifts the design out of the ordinary.

■ The magazine "City Limits" is known for its anarchic style. In the 1983 example, **above**, images were deliberately placed over the type to obscure it and the primary colors in vogue at that time exploded out of the page. The current style, **right**, has "bastardized" typefaces via the computer, destroying their form and design.

■ **Above** A double-page spread from a rather large childrens' book by R. Meal called "Get Fit & Fiddle in the Kitchen." Its approach is very similar to that of Clarks choco, on page 102, in that it's great fun, has lots of color and large readable type. It's just the right thing to encourage children to think healthily about their eating and living habits. It's so well done, I suspect that quite a few adults will take a sneaky read after lights out.

Far left, left and below Banks now realize that they are in the marketplace just as much as anyone else, whether they are selling silk stockings, flashy automobiles or hamburgers. Banks also have a product to sell. The Midland Bank understands this requirement, and like all big banks, they're very anxious to encourage young, first-time investors, students and graduates who will soon have money to save. Just look at these examples – they are tastefully done, have good design and well-balanced color, but they're not stuffy. It is very likely that they will attract young investors.

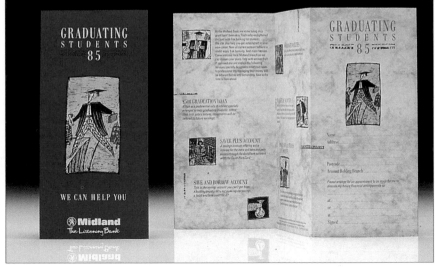

Left It's not only the literature of banks that has changed, the imagery of their exteriors and interiors has also been modernized. In come softer, recessive colors to project friendship, and instil confidence in the potential customer. Note the banners showing their interest in the student market.

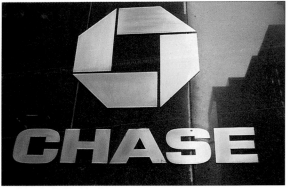

Banking and finance

Banking and finance make an interesting comparison with some of the previous design areas in as much as, although their objective of evoking mood is identical, their actual implementation of color is much narrower and more clearly defined. Most financial institutions will steer clear of strident, bright colors with good reason — they are trying to persuade people that they are serious about looking after their money. So safe colors, mainly of a recessive nature (such as browns, grays and blues), are usually used in a careful attempt to project friendship and instil confidence in the potential customer. However, some banks and other institutions are breaking away from their traditional image to appeal to younger savers, and this new, brighter image is reflected in the colors that advertise them.

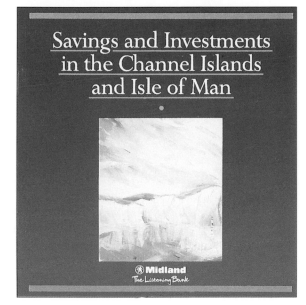

■ **Above** In contrast to their literature for young investors, the design for the Midland Bank's guide to investments in the tax-free Channel Islands and the Isle of Man is aimed at wealthier, more serious investors – the colors and type have been adjusted accordingly

■ **Below** A new brand image for Thorn EMI Lighting by Cope Woollcombe & Partners. The logo is clean and strong, with the design of the 2D echoing the lighting that this company produces. **Below right**, the Omega and Mini-Spot ranges of lighting, also by Thorn EMI, are introduced using a progression of the face used for their 2D logo, this time placing the headlines inside the shape of a fluorescent strip bulb.

■ **Left, below left, right and far right** When an international company is as vast and diverse as Lucas Industries it's not possible to say that any one color sums up their business character. The Lucas house color is green for no other reason that it has always been green, although it has recently been made brighter. The design (by Pentagram UK) of the symbol known as the Lucas diagonal originated in the need for a flexible device suitable for product color-coding. The special characteristics of the stripe are that it is capable of infinite length, can carry or be reversed out of color and is able to wrap around three-dimensional objects. The actual configuration was evolved by cutting a right-angled L (for

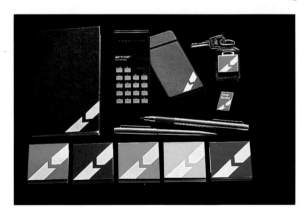

Lucas) in a stripe and moving the two pieces apart. This converted a plain geometric form into a personalized heraldic motif.

THE QUEST FOR KNOWLEDGE

MARCONI TODAY

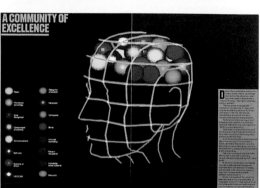

A COMMUNITY OF EXCELLENCE

■ **Left, far left and below left**
The cover and two spreads designed by Lloyd Northover for Marconi's new corporate brochure. The group required a brochure that would show the strength and breadth of the whole company, while emphasizing their new and, in some cases, little-known specialist resources.

The solution is highly visual in treatment with each double-page spread devoted to a single subject. Words are kept to a minimum, set against a brightly colored panel, or reversed out of black. This image of brightness coming out of the dark echoes the radar and ultrasound equipment that the company makes.

Engineering and technology

If banks need to portray friendship and caring, then engineering companies and those involved with high technology must promote themselves as efficient, strong, dynamic and innovative. Their use of color needs to be bright but not flippant. It could suggest their product base, perhaps — a steel company, for example, could use strong gray/blues to promote its business operation.

■ **Above** A brochure designed by Richard Mellor of Sutherland Hawes Design, for Perkson Forging. This company melts down metal to manufacture parts for the automotive industry, a process which is reflected in the bright colors used throughout the brochure to symbolize the changes in color that the metal goes through, from hot yellow to cool blue. The cover of the brochure uses these colors and the company's initials, PF, to create a striking pattern.

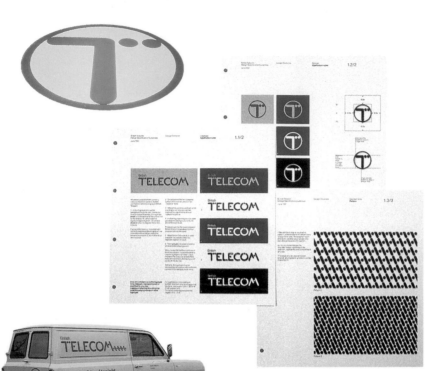

Corporate colors

The importance of the right choice of corporate color can't really be stressed enough, but the logo must be right too. Both must be able to be adapted easily to a range of media which will carry the company's name — from stationery to clothing, shopping bags to store fronts. The colors and lettering must be distinctive enough to survive the competition from other corporate designs, be readily identifiable in any situation, and still project its own, particular image.

■ **Above and right** Color for recognition – this is the purpose of any corporate communications color scheme. British Telecom, the main British telephone company, uses two colors: the dominant color is bright yellow, seen in every British main street on countless service vehicles; the typography and logo is used prominently in blue, the "digital" appearance of the type conveying the sense of high technology. For some literature the color scheme is reversed, with yellow set out of a blue background. These colors are infinitely adaptable to any carrier of the corporate message. As the brochures **above** show, the corporate yellow is strong and stands out well at the head of the design.

■ **Above** The cover and two double-page spreads from the 1985 Annual Report for Warner Communications, designed by Pentagram. Appropriately, for a company involved in films and music recording, the cover is avant-garde, vibrant and entertaining. The script face on the cover and the text spread shows a healthy disregard for formality. The layout of the text spread is clean but striking and good use has been made of contrasting serif and sans serif faces. The solid yellow tint works well as an eye-catcher.

■ **Above and right** Annual report cover and double-page spread for the international company Aidcom. It is a worldwide group of interrelated consultancies specializing in market research, design and new product developments. The design is formal and serious.

Follow the yellow brick road

Color has another role that doesn't rely on its symbolic associations, and this is in the field of information, where its use is as a means of making information clear and legible. In this area the originality of the idea takes second place to the visibility and immediate readability of the message. Because there is such a large range of colors, different hues can be used to make blocks of information distinct from the other information that surrounds them. This function is of tremendous importance in the design of such material as timetables, annual reports, forms, calendars, sign systems and maps.

Most work of this nature can be read and understood to only a small degree when produced in black and white, because the greater the complexity of columns and facts, the harder it is for people to find their way around what they are looking at and comprehend it. But by including colored rules to separate vertical and/or horizontal columns, or colored tints behind selected areas, or by marking out particular items in color, the designer can reduce these problems. Color distinctions are extremely helpful when signs are read from a distance, as are the road signs on a highway that distinguish between minor roads and highways.

I find that the best way to approach complex problems of tabular design is first to conceive the initial concept in monochromatic terms and then

■ **Below** Two simple examples of color use to separate, or pin-point, particular items within the design or text. On the left the various sections of the magazine contents are made easily visible by the use of colored sub-headings. On the right, colored tints behind the type separate additional features from the main body copy.

to introduce secondary elements and colors. It is far easier to assess illegibility objectively in monochrome and then to add other colors one by one to resolve areas of poor legibility and clarity.

Another form of colour "signposting" concerns shop signs. This extremely important visual element informs shoppers immediately of where to purchase their desired commodity. This is particularly important for large chain stores, such as Safeway, Marks and Spencer and Woolworth. They know that as customers move around from town to town, city to city, country to country, on business or vacation, they must be able to pick out their favorite store from the inevitable sea of neon, display and billboards that surrounds any busy shopping area. The corporate color schemes are often designed to be bright for just this purpose.

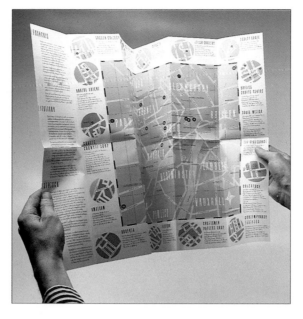

■ **Left and below** Maps and timetables are areas where efficient and well-planned color-coding is essential. Complex timetables must communicate information quickly and clearly to travelers, who are often short of time as they seek their next destination, time and terminal.

33 | a

km	km	treinnummer		5517	5815 2913		1817
0		Amsterdam CS	V	◉ 5 13	◉ 5 33		✕ 6 03
4		Amsterdam MP		◉ 5 19	◉ 5 39		6 08
14		Weesp			② 5 46		6 15
23		Naarden-Bussum			5 54		6 22
23		Bussum Zuid			5 57		6 24
29		Hilversum			6 02		6 30
36		Baarn			6 08		6 36
45		Amersfoort	A		◉ 6 16		✕ 6 43
		treinnummer		315	1615 ⚭ 17		5617
	0	Utrecht CS	V	▣ 5 50	◉ 5 56	◉ 6 23	◉ 6 26
	3	Utrecht Overvecht			5 59		6 29
	9	Bilthoven			6 04		6 34
	12	Den Dolder			6 07		6 37
	16	Soestduinen			6 11		6 41
	21	Amersfoort	A	6 05	6 16	6 37	◉ 6 46
		treinnummer					1817
45	21	Amersfoort	V	6 08	6 18	6 39	✕ 6 49
56	32	Nijkerk			6 26		6 56
63	39	Putten			6 31		7 01
68	44	Ermelo			6 35		7 05
72	48	Harderwijk			6 40		7 10
78	54	Hulshorst					7 15
84	60	Nunspeet			6 47		7 19
93	69	't Harde			6 53		7 25
102	78	Wezep			7 00		7 02
111	87	Zwolle	A	▣ 6 43	◉ 7 07	◉ 7 13	✕ 7 39

▣ maandags en op 27 dec., 2 jan.,
24 april en 1 mei
② Utrecht CS A ◉ 5 43
(via Breukelen, zie tabel 30a)

SUD-EST (suite) 11

				TEE				30	27		28	26		
✕	✕	✕	✕		✕	✕	✕			✕			✕	✕
6 45	7 45	9 25	10 05	13 20	14 30	17 00	PARIS-Gare de Lyon ★ ...	6 d12	6 26	7 27	7 45	8 27	8 30	13 30
9 04	10 09	11 46	12 52	15 39	16 52	19 21	DIJON ★ ...		3 18	3 57	4 29	5 24	5 27	11 07
10 33	11 45	13 31	14 00	17 07	18 40	20 51	LYON-Perrache ★ ...	1 10	1 20	0 08		3 24	3 31	9 26
11 30	12 45	14 43	15 01	18 02	19 40	21 49	VALENCE ★ ...	0 02		22 10				8 14
12 29	13 46	15 55	16 04	19 00	20 39	22 55	AVIGNON ★ ...	22 52	22 55	20 46	23 59			7 05
13 30	14 50	17 02	17 06	19 59	21 43	0 07	MARSEILLE ★ ...	21 48	21 42	19 22	22 30	23 30	23 53	6 00
14 25	16 a00	18 08	17 54	20 49	22 36	1 11	TOULON ★ ...	20 50	20 44	18 23	21 02	22 48	23 02	4 42
16 04	17 a55	20 13	19 58	22 25	0 15	▼	NICE ...	18 41	18 24	16 20	18 50	20 45	21 05	

TEE			✕ 26			27	28	29		✕		✕	✕	TEE	✕
17 37	20 42	20 45		21 46	22 30	22 d57	PARIS-Gare de Lyon ★ ...	13 44	16 50	18 55	19 d50	21 50	22 16	23 35
	23 47	23 50	1 48			1 42	2 25	DIJON ★ ...	14 24	16 29	17 25	19 18	19 56	21 14
21 21				0 09	2 43		4 15	LYON-Perrache ★ ...	9 58	13 50	14 59	17 48	18 30	19 46
22 15		1 44						VALENCE ★ ...	9 15	11 44	13 54	14 17	16 45	17 34	18 51
23 13			4 c35	5 07	6 10	6 30	AVIGNON ★ ...	8 07	10 42	12 54	13 08	15 45	16 35	17 53
0 10	3 15	5b52	5d51	6 20	7 45	7 48	MARSEILLE ★ ...	7 10	9 37	11 55	12 01	14 41	15 35	16 54
1 11	6 10	6 15	6 57	7 23	8 40	8 40	TOULON ★ ...	6 01	8 48	11 04	10 50	13 50	14 49	15 36
	8 07	8 20	9 07	9 40	10 27	10 27	▼ NICE ...		7 10	9 04	9 50	12 07	13 15	13 52

(a) Toulon 15 h 37, Nice 17 h 22 certains jours.
(b) Marseille Blancarde.
(c) Avignon 3 h 07, Marseille 4 h 37, certains jours.

(d) Paris Nord.
(e) Arrivée à 20 h 03 à partir du 20 février 1978.

	✕					✕		✕						TEE
6 00	6 25	8 00	9 08	10 53	13 44	15 17	MARSEILLE ★	6 58	7 43	8 45	9 28	11 45	13 12	13 53
6 40	7 10	8 40	10 06	11 33	14 25	16 00	TOULON ★	6 01	6 54	8 04	8 48	11 04	12 22	13 14
8 36	9 17	10 27			16 04	17 55	▼ NICE			6 15	7 10	9 04	10 20	11 44

TEE	✕		TEE		✕		✕		TEE					TEE
16 50	17 14	18 30	19 25	20 11	21 57	0 15	MARSEILLE ★	15 28	19 05	20 15	21 42	22 39	23 26	23 52
17 28	17 54	19 18	20 06	20 49	22 36	1 11	TOULON ★	14 49	18 23	19 36	21 02	21 55	22 43	23 10
18 58	19 58		22 17	22 25	0 15	▼	NICE	13 15	16 20	18 00	18 50	19 56	20 30	21 13

VOYAGEZ SANS FATIGUE AVEC VOTRE AUTO
UTILISEZ LES **TRAINS AUTOS COUCHETTES**

Right and far right Strangers to large cities always have problems finding their way around. Street and highway signs therefore need to inform quickly and efficiently; color-coding needs to be clear and consistent, and typefaces need to be legible. The most efficient typeface chosen for directional signs is the basic sans serif (Helvetica, with its simple, clear-cut lines is the most common). Just imagine how confusing life would be if all signs were in black and white!

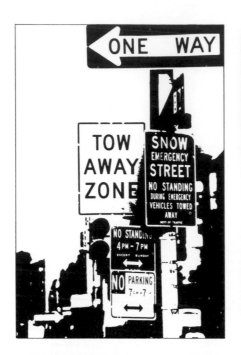

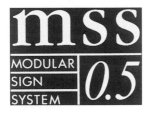

Above and right Sections of folds from a broadsheet which promotes a "Modern Sign System" (logo above) for the HB sign company. Starting at the 5×8" Entrance the broadsheet unfolds, following the arrows, through a series of colorful instructions to reveal the final 8×11" message that promotes the product.

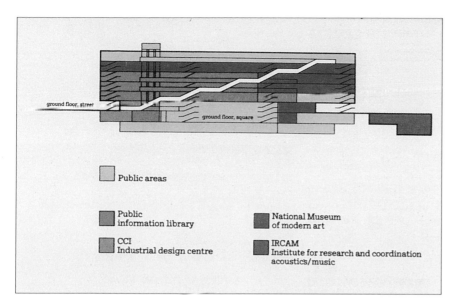

Public areas

Public
information library

CCI
Industrial design centre

National Museum
of modern art

IRCAM
Institute for research and coordination
acoustics/music

■ **Above and right** Further
examples of informative
color-coding. These extracts from
a leaflet explain the various levels
and areas within the Georges
Pompidou Centre in Paris.

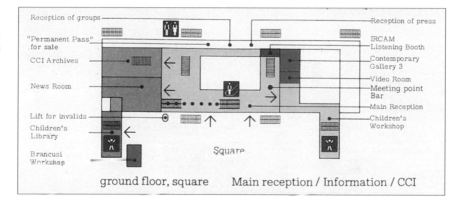

■ **Above** A simple,
easily-understood color-coded
design which explains the major
express routes of the British Rail
system.

■ **Left** In order to achieve
consistency of color-coding for
their vast range of products,
Lucas Industries produced a
series of manuals to explain the
correct implementation of colors
for each of their products.

Any color will do

This is where designers can let their hair down. Gone are the restrictions of having to consider product association, socio-economic groups, value, image, mood, etc. Here color can be pure self-indulgence. If it looks right, it is right, the only rules being those of your own aesthetic criteria. However this freedom itself can pose problems. Many designers find it a bigger handicap than being presented with a tightly controlled brief dictated by detailed market research. These next four images illustrate various examples of free creativity. Although there has ultimately been a client to satisfy, the main feature of these examples is their obvious freedom of expression.

Right A fun design from Tim Girvin Design using words painted in free brush script in lively colors to represent the bunch of flowers.

Above A very colorful design by Lloyd Northover for the promotion of Crillee – a new typeface in the Letraset range of instant lettering. They have cheated a little, as the typeface is spelt with a C, not a K, but the design is still fun.

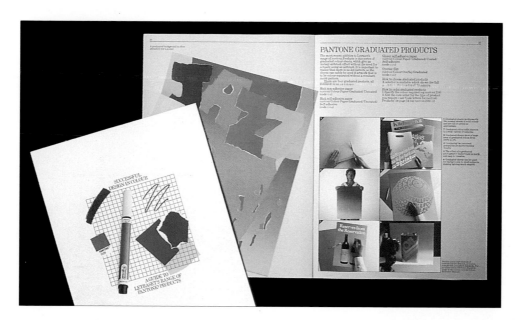

Left These designs by Lloyd Northover, also for the Letraset company, are extracts from a brochure created to promote the Pantone range of colors and products.

Right A spread by the designers Grundy & Northedge which makes very good use of white space and spots of color.

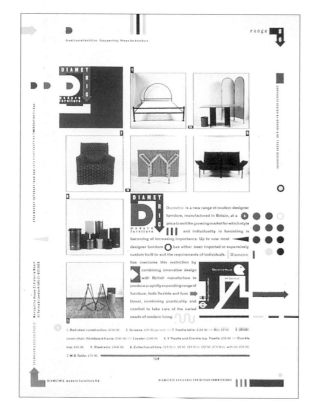

Above The 1987 catalog cover for Quarto, a publishing company, designed by QDOS. The color is restrained with just an occasional touch of bright color here and there.

Cleveland Opera Theater 1983 Tenth Anniversary Season

Above What a fine piece of design. Both self-indulgent and functional, it contrasts the fine calligraphy of Georgia Deaver against the tasteful illustration of the flowers.

Left As mentioned previously, television provides designers with marvelous opportunities for colorful and adventurous typography. This is a fine example of such a titlepiece, by Glazer & Kalayjian, for Katz Sports.

Above These banners, marking 42nd Street in New York, could have been designed in any colors, but none are as striking as the primaries – red, yellow and blue.

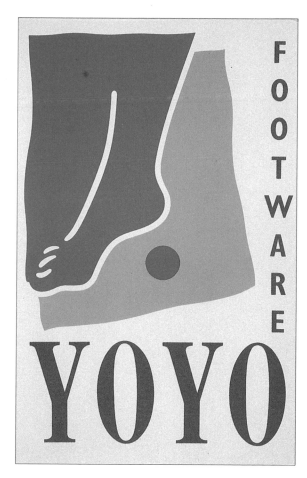

FOOTWARE

YOYO

■ **Above** Coley Porter Bell designed this decorative logo as part of a scheme to promote an in-store range of footwear by Yoyo. Moving well away from what could be termed conventional colors they have used two unusual but successful color combinations.

■ **Right** Color has been used functionally in this layout to identify blocks of text, but it is decorative in the sense that the choice of colors was arbitrary. However, I think the use of color here lacks any subtlety and borders on the crude.

■ **Above** T-shirts now form a very important area of promotion and the typographer can go to town on these designs. If the clothes you wear are a personal statement about yourself this is taking your statements one stage further.

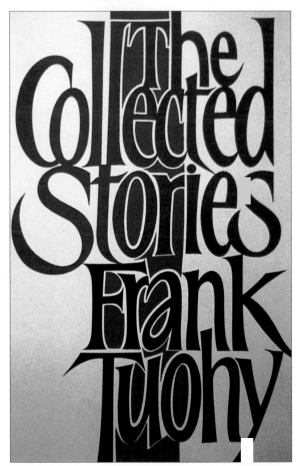

■ **Above** A logo design by Vaughn Wedeen Creative, Inc. for the "Inn on the Alameda." The mirrored cap A contributes well to the decorative nature of this flat three-color design.

Above A book jacket design by Gun Larson for the publisher Alfred A Knopf. The excessive space between the L and O in Louise is well-solved and adds extra dimensions to the decorative nature of the chosen typeface. On the original, both the line shadow around "Louise Bogan" and the word "Elizabeth Frank" are printed in silver, but as the "Louise Bogan" silver is printed next to orange it takes on a gold appearance, adding extra color to the final design.

Left A calendar box set by Trickett & Webb. The cover is purely decorative, evoking a Japanese feel which is associated with the contents of the calendar. There is a very clean use of white space on the actual calendar spreads, which draws attention to the dramatic photography. The red and black vertical blocks add a new dimension to what would otherwise have been a fairly ordinary calendar page.

Above This attractive and tasteful series of cards for Opéra Photographic, designed by Martin Butler, takes its design from collage. The letters are made from torn paper and cut-outs. The colors chosen are perhaps a little too subtle for a photographic company.

Square pegs in round holes

For anyone wishing to become a "professional" professional designer it is certainly necessary that he or she have a working knowledge of type and copyfitting. It is the designer's responsibility to discover in advance whether or not there will be copyfitting problems, and if so, to what extent. With a prior knowledge of such problems the designer has the opportunity of offering a range of solutions and implementing the most appropriate answer to put matters right.

Those who work regularly with copyfitting problems are often required to fit a great deal of copy around all manner of shapes. In fact most typographers relish the challenge of complicated run-arounds (copyfitting around irregular shapes). There is a great deal of pleasure in fitting square pegs into round holes, especially when it works the first time — if only it would more often! But when faced with a mass of copy and illustrative matter where does the typographer start?

There are two interrelated aspects of any design problem, including the text, that need to be discussed and resolved prior to commencement of the work. Simply, they are whether or not to:

(i) design to the supplied copy or,
(ii) write copy to fit the design.

Which actually comes first, design or copy, does not really matter. The answer will depend more on the nature of the job in hand. For example, technical literature will always require a certain amount of copy, regardless of what the designer may wish. This suggests that the copy take preference over design, which will be created appropriate to the text. Conversely, a simple ad with a crisp snappy headline can often be designed first, followed by a request from the designer to the copywriter for x number of words to complement the layout.

There is more than one method of fitting copy into a particular space, and each typographer has his or her own particular favorite. When complicated run-arounds are involved, my own preference is to estimate the type size and leading, have the type set from the galley proofs, produce an accurate tracing of the space allotted to the copy showing the appropriate line breaks, and then have the whole job re-run to fit. It might sound a rather lengthy process, but it does give the typographer total control, although on smaller jobs it can be quicker to work straight from type specimen sheets and trace each word in position on a master layout for the typesetter to follow.

The complex problems of run-around type may now be solvable by the computer, but the use of such equipment is expensive and it can be cheaper to rely on the traditional methods. I mentioned above that my own preference is to order a galley proof of the copy and then to make an accurate tracing indicating the copy run-around. This method does work well, particularly for large jobs, and it makes it reasonably easy to calculate the size and line feed of your type.

The copy should be typed on a standard elite typewriter, and the layout drawn in marker pen to indicate quite clearly where the copy, illustrations and photographs should be positioned. The appropriate transparencies and illustrations should be included so that accurate position and proportions can be calculated for both typesetting and artwork purposes.

First, draw up accurately on a sheet of tracing paper the page size and any internal margins or columns designated by the designer.

Having completed this, mark out the position of the illustrations. You will probably have to trace them up using a visualizing camera, or camera

■ **Left** The first stages of copyfitting: a rough layout with a type mark-up, the type indicated in lines of black felt-tip; a rough layout with the color mark-up; the first galley of set text; and the artwork for the main heading, in bromide.

lucida. This gives you the opportunity of assessing the best proportions and crop for the illustrations. When producing a working tracing for other artists and designers to progress further, try to use a *black* felt-tip pen to indicate the copy, *blue* for the position of artwork and *red* for typographic instructions.

COUNTING THE CHARACTERS

Now to estimate a suitable point size for the type. First produce an accurate character count for each paragraph from your supplied copy. The quickest method, assuming that you have correctly prepared typewritten copy, is with the aid of a standard inch rule. Most typewriters produce either 10 or 12 characters to the inch, so simply measure the length of the average line length, multiply the number of inches by 10 or 12 and then by the number of lines in each paragraph.

Copyfitting tables are available for most typefaces, but their use can be rather longwinded. There is a much simpler method, which only requires your typesetter's sample alphabet sheets and a small pocket calculator. I must point out that it is very important that your reference sheet is supplied by your chosen typesetter; machines do vary, and typeface design can change quite considerably from one manufacturer to another. The wrong spec sheet can easily cause inaccuracies when casting off.

From your specimen sheet assess the size you feel appropriate and measure the length of its lower case alphabet and apply it to this simple equation.

$$\frac{\text{Length of line x 29}}{\text{Length of lower case alphabet}} = \text{Number of characters per line}$$

Why the figure 29? Although there are 26 characters in the English alphabet the letters m and w occur infrequently, whereas small unit characters such as i, l and t occur with greater frequency, therefore the figure of 29 is more accurate. That figure can be reduced if your copy contains an above average quantity of caps and numerals. It's the simplicity of this method that allows the typographer greater flexibility than would normally be found with conventional tables. The beauty of this fraction is that it will work in any unit of measurement, unlike copyfitting tables.

Once you have calculated the number of characters per line it is a simple matter of math to calculate the number of set lines per paragraph. If the copy falls well short or well over simply repeat the exercise with a different point size. With experience you'll find that you will assess the cor-

Right The amount of characters in a line can be estimated by counting the numbers of characters in an inch, and multiplying them by the number of inches in the line of type.

Right The number of characters in a line of set type can also be calculated by referring to the type specimen book. Measure the length of your set line, multiply it by 29 and divide it by the length of the lower case alphabet on your alphabet sheet.

rect size first time with increasing regularity.

First, work out a specific measure for your galley, preferably a width unaffected by the run-around. If the shape is totally free, without any specific measure, you will find it easier to have the galley set to the longest line and work from that. You then need to estimate the area available for text. Working from your chosen measure, calculate the depth that the type area would fill if it were not an irregular shape but a conventional rectangle. This is quite easy to work out. Once you have estimated a proportionately equal rectangular area of copy, work out your type size. This is the size of type you require to fit your run-around; you are now ready to order your galley proof.

To save both time and money, work directly from a first proof; there is no need for your typesetter to correct any keyboard errors at this stage (although they should be marked on the proof), since corrections can be made when the job is re-keyed for the new line endings of the run-around. Having received your galley, simply trace the type, working the copy around the various shapes of the illustration areas until, ideally, you run out of both

■ **Above** To arrive at a rectangle in order to work out your type size in an irregular shape, construct, by eye, a rectangle (y), in which b is equal to the area of a. The resulting rectangle z, which consists of c and a, will be equal in area to c and b, and will be the rectangle you use to calculate your type size.

■ **Left** An alternative to tracing the type around the illustration shapes is to cut up each line of text and fit it around the shapes. You might do this if you were going to show the layout to the client.

■ **Left** The reworked galley has been returned to the typesetter and has now been set as a run-around. It is ready to be pasted down as camera-ready artwork.

space and copy simultaneously.

If the copy falls a bit short, try re-working the type with a little extra leading. This is quite easily assessed with a standard type scale. If the copy falls well under or over, don't panic. Estimate visually the size you think would fit, then reduce or enlarge your proof to your assessed type size with a PMT machine. Make a print and repeat the exercise. If you do not have a repro camera you can re-trace the copy directly from your camera lucida. It's not ideal but it will produce the results you need.

You'll be surprised at how proficient you become with experience, but beware! No matter how long you've been copyfitting there will always be the occasional job that, because of unfortunate word lengths and wordbreaks, just won't fit. When this does occur, see if it is possible for the copywriter to re-phrase some of the text, or ask if the art

director is prepared to accept modifications to the proportions and crops of the illustrative matter. Good graphic design is about teamwork. In the final analysis it is the visual appearance of the finished work that counts.

If your layout contains greater flexibility than the example I've just illustrated, you can avoid much of the tracing work I've described. For example, if your design starts with a run-around and then standardizes to a uniform measure, the copy mark-up can be handled quite simply. Calculate the type size by the method described in the previous example. Then, on your layout, rule where you wish each line of type to be positioned, base line to base line, leaving a uniform gap between the end of each line and the illustration. Measure each line in ems and points, neatly marking the line length of each line on the tracing.

■ **Right** the two examples of copyfitting are well-executed and answer their own particular design objective. The clever feature of the Trickett & Webb example **right**, is the openness of the layout combined with the extremely short measure, which reduces certain lines to just two words. **Far right** is a promotional piece by Ben Casey for the Conway typesetting company, a case where excellence of typography is an obvious prerequisite.

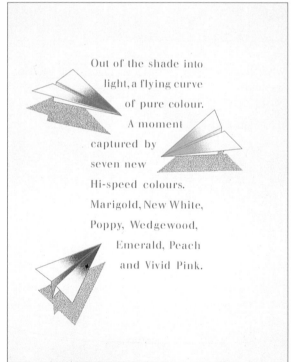

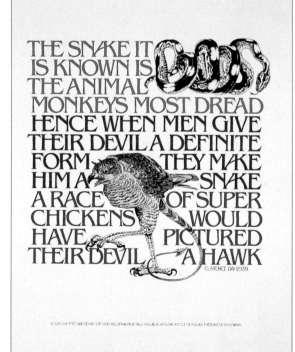

"CORKS"

Around Bovill, Idaho, it's not hard to tell whether a coffee shop is popular with loggers. Just check the floor for puncture marks. ▲ Caulked boots—or "corks," as loggers pronounce it—have steel-spiked soles, which give great traction when walking on wet logs or over steep terrain (but are murder on tile floors). ▲ "Corks" originated in the New England forest region in the early 19th century. Loggers would hammer short spiked nails into their boots to give them better footing when working on the river log drives. Sometime later, traveling shoesmiths went from camp to camp measuring loggers for boots. Each pair was custom-made. The boots were so heavy and solidly constructed that early day loggers claimed that a frozen caulked boot could be a lethal weapon. ▲ Back in camp days, isolated from proper society, loggers weren't always fastidious about grooming. In fact, some postponed doing their wash until their garments took on a life of their own— literally and figuratively. ▲ However, even the most unkempt logger devoted attention to the upkeep of his boots. Boots, after all, meant not only comfort, but safety—not to mention a considerable investment. ▲ On their Sundays off, loggers scraped their "corks" of mud, oiled the leather with bear grease or whale oil to keep it from cracking and replaced loose spikes. ▲ The end of river log drives marked the end of caulked boots as well —except in the Pacific Northwest and Alaska. Here the tradition is carried on because "corks" still offer the best safety in mountainous timberland. ▲ As in years past, Idaho loggers take enormous pride in their "corks." Even today the best "corks" are handmade, with all kinds of special touches for comfort and durability.

To form a rock-solid heel, bootmakers use two outer layers of thick cowhide with a thinner middle layer.

Suede cowhide is frequently used for the exterior of the boot, because it does not cut or nick as easily as smooth leather. Two layers of ½-inch thick cowhide make up the toe area for extra protection. Steel toe guards are not as frequently used because the steel can wear down or cut the leather.

Half-inch wide trim on the soles acts like a bumper, giving more protection to the edges. Hobnails keep the edges from wearing away quickly.

Eyelets and lacing hooks are made from brass, an easily malleable metal.

As in centuries past, the boots have leather laces. Potlatch loggers in Idaho aren't sure why leather is chosen over nylon. However, one forester suggested that it was because after a couple months wear, the laces have stretched long enough to give you an extra pair.

Caulks are machined out of forged steel bars for durability. These sinister-looking spikes, Idaho foresters claim, are a necessity when walking over "buckskin"—i.e., slippery—logs. Made from extremely hard leather, soles are soaked in water. While wet, caulks are driven in. Then soles are dried so the leather shrinks tightly around the steel spikes.

The boot is stitched together with heavy nylon thread, with several rows of stitching at pressure points.

14

15

■ Typographers love the challenge that this type of layout provides and in this instance the designers Jonson Pederson Hinrichs and Shakery have handled the problem with fine skill and judgment. The introduction of the small Christmas trees to denote paragraph endings is first, a nice visual touch, and second, a clever trick to simplify the wrap-around problems. For example, to the right of the boot the word "weapon" ends a paragraph. If the tree device were not used the single word would be left as an orphan at the head of the column which would have been totally unacceptable.

The typesetter can then set each line to your given measure creating the run-around you require.

You can of course use this method for more complex work, but it can be expensive if it doesn't work the first time. Generally speaking, keyboard time is charged at a far higher rate than that for typographers and artists. This is necessary to cover the high investment in typesetting equipment.

WORKING FROM A GRID

For general brochure and leaflet work the starting point for most designers is the formation of a basic grid structure. The grid may be an ideal starting point for most problems, but if it is implemented too rigidly it can cause more problems than it solves. For instance, if the grid structure deems it necessary to preserve a rigid format on each page with illustrative matter of a fixed size and position, it has to be appreciated that there is little freedom to meet a client's demand for that "extra" paragraph to be crammed into the text. Within any basic grid structure it is always good practice to build flexibility into your design. Allow yourself the freedom to vary the crop and proportions of your illustrations, and don't forget white space. The inexperienced designer – and certainly the client – is more often than not afraid of white space. Used intelligently, white space will always allow the design to breathe, be fresh, and most important of all, improve legibility. Within the most basic of grid structures it's surprising how much flexibility can be built into the structure.

So far I've stressed the importance of flexibility within the layout, the intelligent use of white space and the advantages of allowing designs to breathe freely. The possibility of space and flexibility within a design brief is not always available to the typographer. Although good designers and typographers always have in mind the objectives of fresh, readable layouts, how do they achieve such objectives when faced with the large amounts of text required to fit within the tight restrictions of magazine and newspaper layout, for example? The amount of copy into the minimum amount of space — achieved, sadly, at the expense of design and legibility. But this doesn't necessarily have to be the case.

I hope that some of the tips and examples within this appendix will help with possible problems of copyfitting and enable you to bring your own and other designers' ideas to fruition.

■ **Right** This design has become a standard style of layout for upmarket fashion magazines. The photographer was Gilles Bensimon, for Elle magazine.

Glossary

When you're compiling a glossary, the difficulty is not in knowing where to begin, but where to stop. I've tried to restrict this glossary to typographic terms and to terms that the typographer is likely to encounter while dealing with typesetters, artists and designers. *Italic type indicates that the word or term has its own glossary entry.*

A

AA Abbreviation of "Author's Alteration," used to identify any alteration in the text or illustrative matter that is not a printer's error.

Accent A mark added to a letter in certain languages to indicate a change in pronunciation, stress, etc., e.g. acute é, cedilla ç or grave è.

Addendum Matter to be included in a book after the body copy has been set, which is printed separately at the beginning or end of the text.

Advertising rule Rule used to separate one magazine or press advertisement from another.

Align To arrange letters and words on the same horizontal or vertical line.

Alphabet length Horizontal measurement, in points, of the length of the *lower case* alphabet.

Alphanumeric Contraction of "alphabetic" and "numerical" referring to any system that combines letters and numbers.

Ampersand The symbol "&," used as an abbreviation for the word "and."

Arabic numerals Numerals from 1 through 9 and zero (as opposed to Roman numerals), so called because they originated in Arabia.

Arm Horizontal stroke of the characters E and F, which is free on one end.

Artwork All original copy, whether prepared by an artist, camera, or other mechanical means. Loosely speaking, it is any copy to be reproduced.

B

Ascender That part of the lower case letters b, d, f, h, k, l, and t that rises above the *x-height*.

Asterisk The symbol *; usually used to indicate a footnote or to give special emphasis.

Author's alterations See *AA*

Author's proof Marked proofs with typographical errors corrected by the *typesetter*. The author reads them and makes any necessary alterations.

Backslant Typeface that slants backward, i.e. opposite to *italic*, which slopes forward. The effect can be obtained by many headline machines and *computer typesetters*.

Bad break Incorrect end–of–line hyphenation, or a page beginning with either a *widow* or the end of a hyphenated word.

Bad copy Any manuscript that is illegible, improperly edited, or otherwise unsatisfactory to the *typesetter*. Most typesetters charge extra for setting from bad copy.

Banner Main headline across the full width of the page.

Bar Horizontal stroke in the letters A, H, e, t and similar characters.

Base line Imaginary line on which the base of a line of type (excluding *descenders*) rests.

Bastard size Non-standard size of any material used in graphic design.

Black letter Script with angular outlines developed in Germany, which superseded the lighter *Roman* in the 12th century. The term is also applied to types developed from it, such as *Fraktur, Gothic,* and *Old English.*

Blad Sample pages of a book produced in booklet form for promotional purposes.

Bleed Area of plate or print that extends (bleeds off) beyond the edge of the trimmed sheet. Applies mostly to photographs and areas of color.

Block serif Typeface in which the serifs are

of a similar weight to the main stem, as in the Rockwell, Lubalin and Egyptian typefaces.

Blue line Blue, non-reproduceable line, printed or drawn by the artist on artwork as a layout guide for the position of typesetting, artwork, etc. Because the lines are blue they do not show when photographed for platemaking.

Body The *shank* of the type.

Body size Overall depth of the body of a piece of type measured in *points.*

Body text Also called body matter. Regular reading matter, or text, as opposed to *display* or *headline* matter.

Body type Also called *text* type. Ranging normally from 6pt to 14pt, it is generally used for text matter.

Boldface Type of a bold, heavy appearance. Normally a bolder version of the standard weight of type.

Book face Weight of typeface suitable for large areas of text.

Border Continuous decorative design arranged around text or illustration.

Bowl Curved stroke that makes an enclosed space within a character. The bump of a P is a bowl.

Box Item ruled off on all four sides usually with a heavy rule or border.

Brace Sign used to group lines or phrases, it appears as }.

Brackets Marks used to enclose and identify editor's addition to text or parenthetical material within other material already in *parentheses* [ ].

Break for color To indicate or separate the parts of camera-ready artwork (also known as a *mechanical*) for color printing.

Break in copy Term indicating that part of the copy that is missing.

Breakline Short line, usually at the end of a paragraph.

Brochure Pamphlet or other unbound short work with stitched or stapled pages.

Built fraction Fraction that is made up from two or more characters. For example, 7/8 would be made from a 7 followed by a /

followed by an 8, as opposed to a *piece fraction*.

Bullet Dot of any size, used as an ornamental or organizational device.

C

Calligraphy Term comes from the Greek words *kalli* and *graphos*, meaning "beautiful writing." A calligrapher is a person who writes in an elegant traditional style, usually with a calligraphy pen, and sometimes with a brush.

Callout Labels, captions, or numbers used on illustrative work.

Cap Abbreviation for capital letter.

Cap height Height of a capital letter from its base line to the top of the character.

Capital letters, capitals Name of the upper case letters. It derives from the inscriptional letters at the head, or capital, of Roman columns.

Cap-line Imaginary line that runs along the top of the capital letters.

Caps-and-smalls Type set with most or all the initial letters in capitals, and other letters in small caps instead of lower case.

Caption Strictly speaking, the caption is the matter printed as a headline. It is usual, however, to refer to descriptive matter printed underneath an illustration as a caption.

Caret The symbol $\land$, used in proof correction to indicate an insertion.

Carolingian script A 9th-century script developed for the Emperor Charlemagne's revision of grammars, Bibles, church books, etc.

Carry forward To transfer text to the next column or page.

Case fraction Small fractions that can be made up as a single character, e.g. $\frac{3}{8}$.

Cast-off Calculation of how much space a given amount of copy will take in a given type size and measure.

Cast-up Calculation by the printer of the cost of typesetting.

Centered Type placed in the center of a sheet or type measure.

Center point The center point is used, among other things, to indicate syllabications. It can be of any size and is usually centered on the lower case *x-height* of the typeface. When used with caps it should be centered in the middle of the *cap-height*.

Center spread Center design of a brochure or magazine covering both pages.

Central processing unit (CPU) Section of the computer that controls interpretation and execution of instructions.

Chapter heads Chapter title and/or number of the opening page of each chapter.

Character Any single unit of a type *font*, whether it be a letter, numeral or punctuation mark (or space, when calculating a character count).

Character count Calculation of the number of characters in a piece of copy.

Character set See *Font*.

Cicero Continental equivalent of the *pica*, but fractionally larger. Used as a unit for measuring the width or measure of a line of type and the depth of a page. One Cicero = about $\frac{1}{4}$", or 12 *Didot points*.

Clean proof Typesetter's proof free from errors.

Close matter Solid type, set with very few breaks.

Close spacing Type set with very little space between the words.

Close-up Instruction meaning to delete a space, i.e. bring the characters together.

Club line Short line coming at the end of a paragraph; should not occur at the top of a page or column.

Colophon Inscription formerly placed at the end of a book giving the title, printer's name, and place and date of printing. It also refers to a publisher's decorative device.

Column inch Publication measurement based on a space one column wide and one inch deep.

Column rule Light-faced rule used to separate columns.

Combination line and tone Combined block used to reproduce halftone photographs or illustrations with superimposed line letters, figures, diagrams, etc.

Command Part of a computer instruction that specifies the operation to be performed, i.e. the typeface, size, line length, etc.

Comp See *Comprehensive*

Compose To set copy in type. This is done by the *typesetter*.

Compositor Also called the *typesetter*. The operator of the computer typesetter.

Comprehensive Often referred to as a *comp*. An accurate layout showing type and illustrations in position, and suitable as a finished presentation.

Computer typesetter Computer-controlled method of setting type.

Condensed face Typeface with an elongated or narrow appearance and with the letters set very close together.

Contact print Photographic print made by direct contact with the negative, as opposed to enlargement or reduction.

Continuous-tone copy Image with a complete range of tones from black to white, e.g. photographs and paintings.

Contraction Shortening of a word by omitting letters other than the first and last.

Copy Matter to be set in type by the typesetter. Can also refer to any matter for reproduction.

Copyfitting See *Cast-off*.

Counter Inside area of type, such as the inside of the letter "O."

CPS Characters Per Second. Measurement of the output speed of the computer typesetting equipment.

Crop To eliminate part of a photograph or illustration in order that it either fits a given area better or makes a better picture.

Cross-head Sub-section, paragraph heading or numeral printed across the page and often centered in the body of text from which it is separated by one or more lines of space. It usually marks the first subdivision of a chapter.

Cursive Typefaces that resemble handwriting, but without connected letters.

D

Dagger The symbol †; footnote reference mark.

Dash The symbol —. A punctuation mark, usually known as an *em dash* or em rule.

Deadline Time by which copy must be submitted.

Definition Degree of sharpness in a negative or print.

Delete Instruction to take out. The proofreader's mark looks like this

Descender That part of the lower case letters g, j, p, q, y, and sometimes J and f, that falls below the *base line*.

Didot point Continental unit of measurement for type, established by the French typefounder, Firmin A. Didot, in 1775. One Didot point = 0.0148″; one Anglo/American point equals 0.013837″.

Differential spacing Spacing of each character of type according to its individual width.

Digital typesetting Typesetting in which the characters are broken down into a dot formation and set close together to form the actual character.

Diphthong Pair of vowels pronounced as one vowel sound, as in Ca*e*sar.

Discretionary hyphen Hyphen that is keyboarded with the copy, and which may or may not be used in the printed matter.

Display Printed matter given prominence by its size and position. This includes prelims, part and chapter titles, headings, advertisements.

Display type Large typefaces designed for headings, etc. As a general rule sizes above 14pt are regarded as display sizes but this does apply very much to the context within which the type is used.

Dot leaders Series of dots used to guide the eye from one point to another.

Double column Two columns placed side by side.

Double page spread Two facing pages on which matter is continued directly across as if they were one page.

Drop folios Page numbers printed at the foot of each page.

Dropped letter/initial Initial letter covering more than one line of type.

Dry transfer lettering Form of lettering transferred to the page by burnishing each letter off the back of a sheet. It is frequently used by designers and is available in a wide range of typefaces and sizes.

Dummy Prototype of a proposed book, brochure, leaflet, etc. in the correct format. It may take the form of an accurate *visual* complete with the correct paper and bulk.

E

Ear Small stroke projecting from the top of the lower case letter g.

Editing Checking copy for factual accuracy, spelling, grammar, and consistency of style before releasing it to the *typesetter*.

Elite Smallest type size produced by a typewriter. It contains 12 characters per inch as compared to the *pica* typewriter letter which has 10.

Ellipses Three dots (...) indicating an omission, often used when omitting copy from quoted matter.

Em Unit of linear measurement. Often wrongly used as an abbreviation for *pica em*. In a general context it is the square of the type size being set. Its main function is in the specification of indentation for paragraphs, e.g. "indent paragraphs 2 ems."

Em-dash A long dash the width of an *em quad*.

Em leader Horizontal series of dots or dashes, evenly spaced one *em* from center to center.

Em-quad/space Space equal to the square of the type body size, e.g. a 12pt quad/space = 12pts x 12pts, an 8pt quad/space = 8pts x 8 pts.

En A measurement half the width of an *em*.

En-dash A dash the width of an *en*.

End-of-line decisions See *H & J*.

En-quad Same depth as the *em (body size)* but half the width of the *em*.

En-rule A dash approximately half an em rule.

Even smalls Small caps used without full size capitals.

Exception dictionary Portion of the computer's memory in which exceptional words are stored. Exceptional words are those that do not hyphenate along the normal rules of hyphenation. E.g. inkling would become ink-ling, NOT inkl-ing

Expanded/Extended type Wider version of a typeface's standard design.

F

Face Group or family to which any particular type design belongs.

Factor number Copyfitting number given to each composition size and typeface developed by the Monotype Corporation. The factor number expresses an average size of character.

Family Group of typefaces in a series with common characteristics of design, but with different weights, such as *italic*, bold, condensed, expanded, etc.

Fat face Typeface with extensive contrast between the thin and thick strokes.

Figures Arabic figures e.g. 1 2 3 are most commonly used. Roman figures e.g. I II III are used for prelims, chapter heads, part headings, etc.

Film advance Distance by which the film/paper in the photo unit of the computer is advanced between lines.

Filmsetting Process of using photographic means (on film or paper) to produce typesetting. It has almost totally replaced metal setting.

Finished artwork See *Mechanical*

Fine rule A rule of hairline thickness.

First proof Proofs submitted for checking by proofreaders, copy editors, etc.

First revise Proof pulled after errors have been corrected in the first proof.

Fit The space between two or more letters. The fit can be modified by the alteration of the set width.

descenders do not touch, unless a special effect is required.

Misprint A typographical error.

Mixing Combination of more than one style of typeface or point size in a word, line or block of copy.

Modern face Term used to describe the type style developed in the late 18th century. A typeface with vertical stress, strong stroke contrast and unbracketed fine serifs.

N

Numerals, Arabic See *Arabic Numerals.*
Numerals, Roman See *Roman Numerals.*

O

Oblique *Roman* characters that slope to the right, similar to *italic*, but less *cursive*.

Old style Type form originating in the 16th century, characterized by diagonal stress and sloped, bracketed serifs.

Old style figures Also called *Hanging figures.* Numerals that vary in size, some having ascenders and others descenders: 1 2 3 4 5 6 7 8 9 10. As opposed to *Lining figures.*

Open matter Type set with abundant line spacing or containing many short lines.

Ornaments Type ornaments used to embellish page borders, chapter headings, title pages etc.

Orphan (also called widow) Last word of a paragraph that stands at the top of the following page by itself.

Outline letters Open characters made from solid ones by putting a line on the outside edge of a letter.

Overmatter Text matter to be added to existing artwork. See *Callout.*

Overrun To transfer one or more words from the end of one line to the start of the next to improve spacing, to "make" a line, etc.

P

Pamphlet Minor booklet of a few pages.

Page proofs Preliminary print for checking against original manuscript and artwork, for correct color and positioning of tint lays, photographs, etc.

Pagination The numbering of the pages in a book.

Paragraph mark Typographic elements used to direct the eye to the beginning of a paragraph □. Often used when the paragraph is not indented.

Parentheses The symbols [ ] used for punctuation marks or ornament.

Paste-up Positioning of artwork ready for reproduction. See also *Mechanical.*

PE Abbreviation for "Printer's error," as opposed to *AA.*

Peculiars Type characters for non-standard, accent-bearing letters, used when setting certain foreign languages.

Period Punctuation mark indicating the end of a sentence or an abbreviation.

Phototypesetting Also known as photocomposition. The production of text for printing, by projecting type images onto photographic film or paper.

Photostat Facsimile copy of a document — typed, written, printed or drawn.

Pica (em) Typographic measurement equal to 12pts (approximately 1/6th of an inch).

Pi characters Special characters not usually included in a type font, such as special ligatures, accented letters, mathematical signs and reference signs. E.g. $\Omega \sum \prod$.

Piece fraction It comes in three styles: *Built*, made up of three separate characters — two text-size numerals separated by a slash (e.g. 3/4); *Case*, which are small-numbered fractions available as a single character (e.g. ⅜); and *Piece*, which are small-numbered fractions made up of three or more elements: numerator, slash or separating rule, and the denominator.

Point Standard unit of typographic measurement. The American/British point is equal to O.O1383″ (approximately 1/72 of an inch).

Point size Indicated by PT or pt. The overall depth of the typeface including the measure of space above and below the actual letter form.

Portrait A composition or image with a depth greater than its width.

Primary letters *Lower case* letters without *ascenders* or *descenders*, i.e: a c e m n etc.

Proof Impression obtained from an inked plate, stone, screen, block or type in order to check the progress and accuracy of the work. Also called a pull.

Proofreader Person who reads the type that has been set, checking it for correctness of style, spelling, punctuation, etc.

Proofreader's marks Marks made by the proofreader to indicate alterations and corrections to be made on the proof. These symbols are standard throughout the industry.

Q

Quad To space out the blank portion of a line to its full measure. A *hot metal* term that is now more commonly referred to as *flush left, flush right* and *centered.* See *Unjustified type.*

R

Ragged left Text that aligns on the righthand margin only.

Ragged right Text that aligns on the lefthand margin only.

Range Instruction to align the righthand or lefthand edge of a block vertically with the type above or below it. See also *Unjustified type.*

Reader See *Proofreader.*

Reference mark Symbol used to direct the reader from the text to a footnote or other reference. The common marks are as follows:
 * Star or asterisk   § Section   † Dagger
‖Parallels   ‡ Double dagger
¶Paragraph

Register Refers to the correct alignment of pages with the margins in order. Also the correct positioning of one color on another in color printing.

Register marks These are the crosses, triangles and other devices used in color printing to position the paper correctly.

Reproduction proofs Also called Repro. High-quality proofs on art paper, which can be used as artwork.

Rivers Streaks of white spacing in the text, produced when spaces in consecutive lines of type coincide.

Revise Change in instruction that alters the copy in any stage prior to final artwork.

Roman Name often applied to the Latin alphabet as it is used in English and other European languages. Also used to identify vertical type as distinct from *italic*.

Roman numerals Roman letters used as numerals until the 10th century A.D. I, II, III, IV, etc.

Rough A sketch that gives a general idea of the size and position of the various elements of a design.

Rule Line used for a variety of design effects including borders, separating lines and boxes from the text. Rules can also be dotted, dashed or decorative.

Run Number of copies to be printed.

Run-around Text that fits closely around an irregular shape.

Run-in Setting of type without paragraph breaks, or the insertion of new copy without making a new paragraph.

Running head Line of usually small type which repeats a chapter heading at the top of a page.

Run on Instruction for text to be continous without a new paragraph. A run-on chapter is one that does not begin on a new page.

Running text Also referred to as *straight matter,* or *body text.* The text of an article or advertisement as opposed to *display type.*

S

Sans serif Typeface without serifs, usually without stroke contrast.

Script Typeface designed to imitate handwriting.

Serif Small terminal stroke at the end of the main stroke of a letter.

Set Refers to the width of a body of type. Also used as an instruction to a typesetter.

Set close Describes type set with the minimum of space between the individual characters and words.

Set solid Refers to type set without any extra *leading.*

Set-width Also called set size, or *set.* The width of each individual character within a *font.* This space, measured in units, can be increased or decreased to adjust the letter spacing.

Shank *Body* of the type.

Shoulder The flat surface on a type above and below the face.

Small capitals Capital letters that are smaller than the standard and usually aligned with the *x-height* of the typeface, i.e. SMALL CAPITALS.

Solid Type set with no leading.

Spec A specification of the size, leading and face of a body of text, for the typesetter.

Spine Main curved stroke of a lower case or capital S.

Spur Small projection off a main stroke: found on many capital G's.

S.S. Abbreviation for same size. Also indicated S/S.

Star Typographical *ornament,* also an incorrect name for an asterisk.

Stat See *Photostat.*

Stem Main heavy vertical element in a letter.

Stet Latin word meaning "let it stand," written in the margin in proof corrections to cancel a previously marked correction.

Stickup initial *Display* letter that base-aligns with the first line of text.

Straight matter *Body type* set in straight rectangular colums with little or no typographic variation.

Stress Direction of thickening in a curved stroke.

Stroke Straight or curved line.

Style See *House Style.*

Subheading Heading for a division of a chapter, paragraph, etc.

Subtitle Phrase, often explanatory, that follows a title of a book.

Superior letters or figures See *Superscript.*

Superscript Small symbol, numeral or letter that prints above the *x-height* and to the side of another character as in 3₄. Also called superior letter or figure, particularly when used to refer to a citation source.

Swash letters Italic types with calligraphic flourishes.

T

Tabular work Type matter set in columns.

Tail Descender of Q or short diagonal stroke of the R; alternatively the margin at the bottom of a book.

Tail piece Design at the end of a section of a chapter or book.

Terminal End of a stroke not terminated with a *serif.*

Text *Body* copy of a page or book, as opposed to headings.

Text type Main *body type,* usually smaller in size than 14pt.

Tint Photomechanical reduction of a solid color by screening.

Title page Righthand page at the front of a book that bears the title, the names of the author and publisher, and sometimes the place of publication and other relevant information.

Titling Headline type which is only available in capitals.

Transfer type See *Dry transfer lettering*.

Transitional Type forms invented in the mid-18th century, which are neither Old Style nor Modern. They include Fournier and Baskerville.

Transpose To change the order of the letters, words or lines.

Transposition Common typographical error in which the letters are incorrectly placed, i.e. "tihs" instead of this.

Trim size Final size of a printed work after trimming. When preparing artwork allowance must always be made for trim.

Type Letters of the alphabet and all the other characters used singly or collectively.

Type area Area of the page designated to contain text and illustrative matter.

Type family Range of typeface designs that are variations of one basic style of design. Thus we have Helvetica bold, light, light italic, condensed, etc.

Type mark-up See *Mark-up*.

Typescript Typed *manuscript*.

Typesetter Person who sets type, or a shortening of "computer typesetter."

Typesetting Copy produced by the computer typesetter.

Type size There are two different methods of defining type size: by the height of the capital letter (see *Key size*), and by the typeface's overall depth measured in terms of the metal block on which the type used to sit in *hot-metal setting*.

Typestyle Variation within a typeface: medium, bold, italic, condensed, etc.

Typographer Person who designs the typographical layout of a proposed printed work. Also a designer of typefaces.

Typography The study of type.

U

U & l.c. Abbreviation of *upper & lower case*.

Uncial Hand-drawn book face used by the measured in units and are the basis for the Romans and early Christians, typified by the heavy, squat form of the rounded O.

Underscore A rule directly below a line of type.

Unit Variable measurement based on the division of the *em* or *set size* into equal increments.

Unitization Designing the *font* characters to width groups. The width groups are counting mechanism of the computer typesetting equipment. Width units can be based on the *em* or the *set size* of the font.

Unit system Counting method first developed by Monotype and now used by some typewriters and all computer typesetting systems to measure, in units, the width of the individual characters and spaces being set. By counting the total accumulated units the computer can determine the measure when the line is ready to be justified, and determine how much space is left for justification.

Unit value Fixed unit width of individual characters.

Unjustified type Lines of type set to different lengths aligning to the left or right.

Upper case Capital letters of a typeface i.e. A, B, C, etc.

V

Visual See *layout*.

W

Weight Degree of boldness of a typeface. Most typefaces are designed in light, medium and bold. These are known as the different weights

White space reduction Reduction of space allocated to the characters.

Widow Single word at the end of a paragraph left on a line of its own. Widows can often be avoided by editing or adding extra copy to lengthen the last line. Also the end of a hyphenated word, such as -ing.

Word break Device of hyphenating a word between syllables so that it can be split into two sections to regulate line length in a text.

Word spacing Adding or reducing space between words to complete justification.

Wrong font Indication that a letter of the wrong size or *font* has been set by mistake. It is abbreviated as w.f.

X

X-height Height of the *lower case* letters without either *ascender* or *descender*.

Z

Zip-a-tone Trade name for a series of screen patterns imprinted on clear sheets. Available in dot, line or stipple form.

Index

Page numbers in *italic* refer to illustrations and captions.

Acknowledgements

p12-13: Bob Farber; **p14:** *top,* Ursula Dawson, London; *bottom right,* Victoria & Albert Museum, London; **p15:** *top,* Peter Thompson; *bottom,* Georgia Deaver, San Francisco, California; **p16:** *top left,* David Harris; *top right,* Tony Geddes; *center,* David Quay; **p17:** *top left and bottom,* Tim Girvin Design, Inc., Seattle, Washington; *top right and top,* Minale, Tattersfield & Partners Ltd, London; *center above,* W Photo, London; *center below,* Vaughn/Wedeen Creative, Inc, Albuquerque, New Mexico; **p18:** *top right,* DRG Records: Art Director John de Vries; *bottom left,* Foote, Cone & Belding, London: Designer Steve Grime: Illustrator Paul Sample; *bottom right,* Paul Peter Piech (detail); **p19:** *top,* Michael Beaumont; *center left,* Grundy & Northedge, London; *center right,* The Partners Ltd, London: Art Director Aziz Cami: Designer Stephen Gibbons: Illustrators Stephen Dew, Line & Line; *below,* The Yellow Pencil Company Ltd, London; **p22:** Conway Group Graphics Ltd, London; **p23:** Herb Lubalin; **p25:** Robert Wakeman, N W Ayer Inc., New York; **p27:**

Robert Wakeman, N W Ayer Inc., New York; **p28:** *top left, top right, center left,* Minale Tattersfield & Partners, Ltd. London; *center,* Coley Porter & Bell & Partners, London; *bottom left,* Trickett & Webb Ltd, London; **p29:** Minale, Tattersfield & Partners, London; **p30:** *top,* Pentagram UK, London; *bottom,* Trickett & Webb Ltd, London; **p31:** *top left, top center, top right,* Trickett & Webb Ltd, London; *bottom right,* The Partners Ltd, London: Art Director Nick Wurr: Designer Clare Boam: Illustrator Nick Brownfield; *bottom left,* The Partners Ltd, London: Art Director Aziz Cami: Designer Karen Wilks; **p32:** The Artist's and Illustrator's Magazine, London; **p33:** *left,* Lloyd Northover Ltd, London; *right,* Case Associates, Toronto, Canada: Designer Mark Walton: Artist Julius Ciss: Writer Pamela Frostad; **p34:** Lynx, Dunmow, Essex, England; Photography David Bailey; **p35:** *left,* Appleton Design, Hartford, Connecticut: Art Director/Designer/Typographer Robert Appleton; *center top and top right,* Grundy & Northedge, London; *center bottom,* Tandem Studios, Salt Lake City, Utah: Designer Daniel Reusch; **p36:** Vaughn/Wedeen Creative, Inc., Albuquerque, New Mexico: Art Director/Designer/Illustrator Steven Wedeen: Copywriter Susan Blumenthal; **p37:** *top,* Pentagram UK, London; *bottom,* Saatchi & Saatchi Compton Ltd, London: Art Director Paul Arden: Photographer Richard Avedon: Copywriter Tim Mellors: Typographer Roger Kennedy; **p38:** U.&l.c., New York: Illustrator Gina Shartleff: Writer Marion Muller; **p44:** Robert Wakeman, N W Ayer Inc., New York; **p45:** Grundy & Northedge, London; **p47:** *left,* Redmond Fugate Amundson Rice & Ross, Richmond, Virginia; *right,* Robert Wakeman, N W Ayer Inc., New York; **p49:** *top left,* Robert Wakeman, N W Ayer Inc., New York; *bottom,* Corporate Graphics, New York: Typography/Design Bennett Robinson, Paul Zographos; **p51:** Robert Wakeman, N W Ayer, Inc., New York; **p52:** Olympia & York Developments, Toronto, Canada: Art Director Simha Fordsham: Designers Nancy Leung, Jonas Tse; **p53:** *top,* The World of Interiors Magazine, London; *bottom,* The Yellow Pencil Company Ltd, London; **p54:** Robert Wakeman, N W Ayer Inc., New York; **p55:** *top left,* Glazer & Kalayjian Inc., New York: Typography/Design: Vasken Kalayjian; *top right and bottom,* Pentagram UK, London; *right,* Richard Mellor, London; **p61:** *left,* Chermayeff & Geismar Associates, Inc., New York: Art direction, Design and Illustration Steff Geissbuhler; *bottom right,* Pentagram UK, London; **p62:** Vaughn/Wedeen Creative, Inc., Albuquerque, New Mexico; **p63:** *top left and bottom right,* Vaughn/Wedeen Creative, Inc., Albuquerque, New Mexico; *top right,* Grundy & Northedge, London; *bottom left,* Cope Woollcombe & Partners, London; **p64:** Vaughn/Wedeen Creative, Inc., Albuquerque, New Mexico; **p65:** *top,* Seymour Robins Design, Sheffield, Mass; *bottom left,* Pentagram UK, London; *center top and bottom right,* Artist's and Illustrator's Magazine, London; **p67:** *top,* Brown Design Group, Providence, Rhode Island: Designer/Typographer Allen Wong; *bottom,* Crucial Books, London; **p68:** i-D magazine, London; **p69:** *top,* Miller Judson & Ford, Inc., Houston, Texas: Art Director/Designer Blake Miller: Photographer Wayne Jesperson; *bottom left and bottom right,* Vaughn/Wedeen Creative, Inc., Albuquerque, New Mexico; **p71:** Canon (UK) Ltd, Wallington, Surrey, England; **p72:** The Post Office, Great Britain; **p73:** Grundy & Northedge, London; **p76:** J. Walter Thompson Co. Ltd, London: Photographer Max Forsythe: Art Director/Designer Luciana Carta: Copywriter Geoff Weedon: Typographer Trevor Slabber; **p77:** *top right,* Pentagram UK, London; *center,* David Davies Associates, London; *bottom left,* Minale Tattersfield & Partners Ltd, London; *bottom right,* Trickett & Webb Ltd, London; **p80:** *top and bottom,* Tim Girvin Design, Inc., Seattle, Washington; *center,* Minale, Tattersfield & Partners Ltd, London; *bottom,* David Davies Associates, London; **p82:** *top and center right,* Coley Porter Bell & Partners, London; *center left,* David Davies Associates, London; *bottom,* Lloyd Northover Ltd, London; **p83:** *top left,* Minale, Tattersfield & Partners Ltd, London; *top right,* Pentagram UK, London; *bottom left,* Quarto Publishing Plc, London; *bottom right,* Vaughn/Wedeen Creative, Inc., Albuquerque, New Mexico; **p84:** *top right,* Lloyd Northover Ltd, London; *bottom left,* The Partners, Ltd, London: Art Director David Stuart: Designers Shaun Dew, Clare Boam; *bottom center,* M & R Martini Rossi Ltd, UK; **p84-85:** *bottom left,* Fitch & Company Plc, London; **p85:** *top left,* Minale, Tattersfield & Partners Ltd, London; *top right and bottom right,* Richard Mellor, London; **p86:** *top,* T.B.W.A. Ltd, London: Creative Team John Knight; *bottom,* Vaughn/Wedeen Creative Inc., Albuquerque, New Mexico; *top right,* J. Walter Thompson Co. Ltd, London: Art Director Annie Carlton: Photographer David Fairman: Posterization Gilchrist Studios; *center right,* Social Democratic Party, UK; *bottom left,* Minale, Tattersfield & Partners Ltd, London; *bottom right,* The Labour Party, UK: Designer Mike Jarvis; **p90:** *top,* Travis Dale & Partners, London; *bottom left,* Fitch & Company, London; *bottom right,* Lloyd Northover Ltd, London; **p91:** *top right,* Quintet Publishing Plc, London; *bottom left,* Pentagram UK, London; *bottom right,* Minale, Tattersfield & Partners Ltd, London; **p92:** *top left, top center and center,* David Davies Associates, London; *top right,* Minale, Tattersfield & Partners Ltd, London; *bottom,* The Worthington Design Co, London; **p93:** *top,* Richard Mellor, London; *center,* Vaughn/Wedeen Creative Inc., Albuquerque, New Mexico; *bottom left,* Trickett & Webb Ltd, London; *bottom right,* Minale, Tattersfield & Partners Ltd, London; **p94:** *top left,* Minale, Tattersfield & Partners, Ltd, London; *top right,* Quarto Publishing Plc, London; *center left,* Fitch & Company Plc, London; *center,* Vaughn/Wedeen Creative Inc., Albuquerque, New Mexico; **p95:** *top left,* Cope Woollcombe & Partners, London; *top center,* Coley Porter Bell & Partners, London; *top right and center,* Minale, Tattersfield & Partners Ltd, London; *bottom left,* Grundy & Northedge, London; **p96:** *top center and bottom,* Coley Porter Bell & Partners, London; *right,* Fitch & Company Plc, London; **p97:** *top,* Fitch & Company Plc, London; *bottom right,* Georgia Deaver, San Francisco, California; *bottom left and bottom center,* Minale, Tattersfield & Partners Ltd, London; **p98:** *top,* The Ian Logan Design Company, London: Designer/Typographer Alan Coleville: Illustrator Brian Cook; *bottom left,* John Brimacombe & Co., London; *bottom right,* Minale, Tattersfield & Partners Ltd, London; **p99:** *top left, top center, center, right, and bottom right,* Coley Porter Bell & Partners, London; *bottom left,* Saatchi & Saatchi Compton Ltd, London: Typographer David Wakefield: Art Director Stewart Howard: Copywriters Rod Lyons/David Bourne; **p100:** *top left,* Fisher, Ling & Bennion Ltd, Cheltenham: Designer Bill Jones; *right,* Pentagram UK, London; *bottom,* Lloyd Northover Ltd, London; **p101:** *top and bottom,* Trickett & Webb Ltd, London; *center left,* Lloyd Northover Ltd, London; *center right,* Minale, Tattersfield & Partners Ltd, London; **p102:** Pentagram UK, London; **p103:** *top left and center right,* Fitch & Company Plc, London; *center left,* Grundy & Northedge, London; *bottom,* Bartle Bogle Hegarty, London; **p104:** Lloyd Northover Ltd, London; **p105:** *top left,* Expression Design, London; *top right,* Field Wylie & Co, Ltd, London: Photography Andy Willis; *center,* Thumb Design Partnership, London: Designer/Typographer Nick Pollitt; *bottom left,* Saatchi & Saatchi Compton Ltd, London: Art Directors Derek Miller, Noel Farrey: Designer Roger Pearce: Copywriters James Lowther, Richard Myers & Roger Pearce; **p106:** *top,* Glazer & Kalayjian Inc., New York; *center left,* Kruddart/Muscle Films, London: Design Nicola Bruce, Michael Coulson; *center right,* Kunst Co, London: Designer Martin Hucksford; *bottom,* Minale, Tattersfield & Partners ltd, London; **p107:** *top left,* Grundy & Northedge, London; *top right,* Hyper Kinetics Ltd London; *center,* Deutsche Grammophon production: Design Gerhard Noack; *center right and bottom,* Vaughn/Wedeen Creative, Inc., Albuquerque, New Mexico; **p108:** *top,* Pentagram UK, London; *bottom,* Elle magazine, London; **p109:** *top left and top right,* Quarto Publishing Plc, London; *center left and bottom,* City Limits, London; *center right,* Roman Meal Company, Tacoma, Washington; **p110:** *top left, top right, bottom right,* David Davies Associates, London; *bottom left,* Fitch & Company, London; **p111:** *top left,* Allied International Designers Ltd, London; *bottom left,* David Davies Associates, London; **p112:** *top,* Cope Woollcombe & Partners, London; *center left, bottom left, bottom right,* Pentagram UK, London; **p113:** *top left,* Lloyd Northover Ltd, London; *right,* Sutherland Hawes Design, London: Designer Richard Mellor; *bottom,* Pentagram UK, London; **p114:** *top left, top center, center left,* Banks & Miles, London; *bottom,* Cope Woollcombe & Partners, London; **p115:** *top,* Pentagram UK, London; *center and bottom,* Allied International Designers Ltd, London; **p116:** *bottom left,* Elle magazine, London; *bottom right,* "Skald" magazine, Pentagram; **p117:** *top,* Trickett & Webb Ltd, London; *bottom right,* The French railway, SNCF; **p118:** *top right,* Michael Beaumont; *center left and bottom,* Minale, Tattersfield & Partners Ltd, London; **p119:** *top left and center,* Centre Georges Pompidou, Paris; *top right,* British Rail/InterCity; *bottom,* Pentagram UK, London; **p120:** *right,* Lloyd Northover Ltd, London; *left,* Tim Girvin Design Inc., Seattle, Washington; **p121:** Lloyd Northover Ltd, London; *bottom right,* Grundy & Northedge, London; *right,* QDOS Design Ltd, London; **p122:** *right,* Georgia Deaver, San Francisco, California; *bottom left,* Glaser & Kalayjian Inc., New York; **p123:** *left,* Coley Porter Bell & Partners, London; *bottom,* "Crafts" magazine, London; **p124:** *top,* The Worthington Design Co. London; *center,* Vaughn/Wedeen Creative, Inc., Albuquerque, New Mexico; *bottom,* David Gatti, New York; **p125:** *top left,* Alfred A Knopf: Typography/Design Gun Larson, Klagstorp, Sweden; *top right,* Opera Photographic Ltd, London: Designer Martin Butler; *bottom,* Trickett & Webb Ltd, London; **p130:** *left,* Conway Group Graphics, London: Design and lettering Ben Casey: Illustrations Will Rowlands; *right,* Trickett & Webb Ltd, London; **p131:** Jonson Pedersen Hinrichs & Shakery, San Francisco, California; **p132:** Elle magazine, London: Photography Gilles Bensimon; **p133:** *top,* Lowe Howard-Spink Narschalk, London: Art Director Alan Waldie: Copywriter Adrian Holmes: Illustrator Roy Knipe: Typographer Brian Hill; *bottom,* B.B. Needham Worldwide, New York: Designer David Garcia: Writer Mike Rogers: Photographer Jim Young.

Quarto would like to thank Mick Hill and Ursula Dawson. We would also like to thank those companies who so willingly sent us transparencies and artwork, and who granted us clearance of their copyright. Every effort has been made to obtain copyright clearance for the illustrations featured in this book, and we apologize if any omissions have been made.